THE OBEDIENCE ALGORITHM

How to Control Anyone and Make Them Call It Freedom

Dominic Rourke

They'll obey. And call it freedom

Table of Contents

Introduction: Why Obedience Is the Only Metric That Matters

The Hidden Architecture of Human Compliance

People think obedience is rare. In reality, it's the default.

The illusion of autonomy is one of the most powerful myths modern humans cling to. They believe they choose, decide, and act based on personal logic and values. But under pressure—social, emotional, environmental—the vast majority fold into the structure handed to them. They comply, not because they want to, but because the system is engineered in such a way that not complying feels disorienting, unsafe, or simply unnatural.

This is the architecture. And most people are already inside it, whether they know it or not.

Obedience doesn't begin at the moment of a command. It begins long before—through signals, priming, emotional climate, and perceived authority. When someone follows your instructions, it's not because of what you said in that moment. It's because of what the system around that moment has conditioned them to accept.

That system has rules. And if you understand them, you can trigger compliance predictably, without needing to convince, persuade, or even be liked.

The Illusion of Choice

When people are given options, they believe they're exercising free will. But almost every option they choose has been pre-filtered, framed, and biased by what's been shown to them beforehand. Social science has proven this over and over: the first exposure, the perceived consequence, the framing of a question—these all shape the decision more than internal belief.

The question isn't "Will they obey me?" The question is "How many of their existing behaviors are already compliance in disguise?"

Look around.

People obey traffic lights, app notifications, workplace hierarchies, political labels, trending hashtags, lifestyle norms, spiritual mantras, even marketing slogans. They wear them like badges of honor and think they're choosing them freely. But behind all of it is an invisible hand. The tone was set. The boundaries were drawn. The behavior was funneled.

That same funnel can be constructed by you.

Command as Structure, Not Force

Most amateurs think compliance is about being louder, more aggressive, more demanding. That's weakness. Loudness is what people resort to when the structure of obedience has failed.

True compliance doesn't need pressure. It needs inevitability.

It's built like scaffolding around the target's mind—carefully designed touchpoints that make disobedience seem illogical or even dangerous. Not because you've threatened them, but because the emotional cost of resistance is too high. You've made compliance feel like the only sane option.

This isn't just about psychology. It's architecture. It's design.

Compliance emerges from invisible factors that shape perception. Things like:

- The order of exposure
- The emotional state at the moment of decision
- The perceived social risk of disobedience
- The cognitive load already occupying their mind
- The symbols of authority present in the environment

These variables don't operate in isolation. They converge. And when you align them correctly, a command doesn't feel like a demand—it feels like an instruction embedded inside reality itself.

That's when people obey without thinking.

That's the goal.

You're not trying to dominate people. You're trying to make resistance structurally irrelevant.

Fear, reward, and identity are not just motivators. They are the pillars that uphold the architecture of compliance. Every system that induces obedience—governments, religions, corporations, cults—uses these three. Some do it with intention. Others stumble into it. But the result is always the same. Behavior that feels internally driven but is externally engineered.

Fear is the fastest trigger. It short-circuits thought. When the cost of disobedience is perceived as pain, loss, or rejection, most people don't stop to analyze. They react. Their nervous system makes the decision for them. This is why totalitarian regimes don't need to arrest everyone. They only need to make the *idea* of disobedience feel dangerous. The rest handles itself.

Reward comes next. It's what people chase when fear is low. Promise approval, access, status, or pleasure, and people will lean in. But more than the reward itself, it's the anticipation that drives compliance. The dopamine spike doesn't happen when they receive the reward. It happens just before—when they expect it. That expectation is the real tool. Use it correctly, and they will follow your lead just to stay in proximity to possibility.

Then there is identity. The deepest structure of all. If you make obedience part of who they believe they are, you no longer have to command them. They'll enforce it themselves. This is why cults are so effective. They don't need to control every action. They control the identity layer. The moment someone thinks, "This is who I am," you've locked in obedience at the level of self-definition.

These levers are not new. They're ancient. But what makes them powerful in your hands is not that you understand them—it's that you can now deploy them with precision, without apology.

Most people use these dynamics by accident. They hope fear will work. They guess what might look like a reward. They try to get someone to "see things differently." But the real strategist builds the structure from the ground up. He creates the emotional climate before the command. He installs the triggers before they're needed. He lets the subject walk into the trap thinking it was their idea.

That's how the system works best. When the target believes they're acting freely. When they say yes and think they meant it. When they submit and convince themselves it was the rational thing to do.

This is what the hidden architecture makes possible.

It's not enough to know how to give an order. Anyone can bark a command. But only those who understand how the environment, the emotional landscape, the timing, and the implied consequence work together can get others to obey without resistance, without drama, without even realizing they've obeyed.

This is control at the structural level. It's quiet. It's invisible. And it's far more dangerous than brute force.

The rest of the book will teach you how to build this structure deliberately. You'll learn to prime their emotions, seed your authority, collapse resistance through language, and create self-reinforcing loops that make disobedience feel unnatural.

But none of that matters if you don't grasp this core idea:

Obedience is not the result of charisma. It's the result of architecture.

And now that you've seen the blueprint, you're no longer playing their game. You're rewriting it.

The Failure of Persuasion: Why Influence Isn't Enough

Persuasion is celebrated because it makes people feel civilized. It suggests mutual agreement, the meeting of minds, the elegant art of rhetoric. But what it really is—at least in the way most people practice it—is a negotiation with uncertainty. A gamble. A way of saying, "Here's what I want, but it's up to you."

That mindset has no place in real control.

If you rely on persuasion, you're depending on someone else's internal world to cooperate with your agenda. You're hoping they see it your way, hoping they respond to reason, hoping they agree. The problem isn't that persuasion never works. The problem is that it's unstable, unpredictable, and always subject to interpretation. You may convince someone today, only to find them slipping back into resistance tomorrow. There's no anchor. No override.

Influence sounds stronger. It implies that you've penetrated deeper into their psychology, nudged them, shaped their thinking. And in a sense, it's a step closer to power. But influence still carries risk. It still depends on permission. It still dances around the idea of force, trying to remain subtle enough not to offend, but strong enough to move.

What neither persuasion nor influence offers is certainty. Neither one guarantees action. And for a strategist who wants control, not consensus, that's unacceptable.

Command bypasses the need for agreement. It doesn't seek validation. It doesn't ask for a reaction. It inserts itself into the behavioral system like a code, and it runs. The subject may rationalize it afterward, explain it to themselves, even believe they made the choice. But the action came from you. It wasn't shared. It was delivered.

This is where most persuasion-based models collapse. They aim for hearts and minds. They try to appeal to values, beliefs, logic. But obedience doesn't live in those domains. It lives in structure. In triggers. In the way the human nervous system defaults under pressure, uncertainty, hierarchy, and threat.

The more emotionally involved someone is in the decision, the less stable that decision becomes. Emotions change. States shift. What seems like agreement now can turn into regret, doubt, or defiance hours later. That's the hidden failure in persuasion: even when it lands, it doesn't last.

Obedience does. Not because it resonates with someone's heart, but because it locks into their operating system.

Persuasion respects the individual's sovereignty. Command deletes it.

If that makes you uncomfortable, you're not ready for control. But if that excites you, keep going.

The tools of persuasion—stories, metaphors, logic, emotional appeal—aren't useless. They can still be used tactically. But not to ask. Not to convince. To destabilize. To soften the field. To lower resistance just long enough to install the command.

This shift in thinking is critical. You're not persuading because you respect their will. You're persuading so that their defenses are down when the real input is delivered.

In other words, persuasion is no longer the goal. It's the disguise.

When a command is issued correctly, it bypasses the conscious mind. It doesn't ask for interpretation. It doesn't trigger debate. It lands in the nervous system like a default setting. It tells the body, not the intellect, what to do. That's why commands work under pressure when persuasion falls apart. Persuasion needs cooperation. Command exploits reflex.

Look at any environment where control is non-negotiable: the military, cults, elite private institutions, crisis response teams. Persuasion is not the method used to drive compliance. They don't have time for it. What they rely on is conditioning, hierarchy, tone, and pre-installed authority. The system is designed so that obedience feels automatic. It doesn't matter how intelligent or resistant someone is. The structure overrides the opinion.

This is the flaw in most communication training. It teaches people how to be liked, how to be convincing, how to build rapport. But being liked is weak currency when your goal is dominance. The people who follow you because they like you will leave when they don't. The people who follow because the structure makes disobedience feel wrong—those are the ones who stay.

Obedience is not about charm. It's about inevitability. The subject complies because the conditions you've shaped around them make resistance feel unnatural. You've reduced the complexity of choice. You've taken away the friction. You've created a loop where the fastest path forward is the one you chose for them.

To the outsider, it may look like persuasion. It may sound polite, even collaborative. But beneath the surface, the machinery is different. You've pre-calculated their response. You've eliminated variables. You've installed mental and emotional consequences that make disobedience feel unsafe, disloyal, or pointless.

That's the true distinction between persuasion and command. Persuasion is a gamble on free will. Command is the deletion of it.

Most people won't see the difference. That works in your favor. They'll think they're being influenced. They'll feel clever for agreeing with you. They'll describe you as charismatic or insightful. Let them. Their perception of what's happening has nothing to do with the result. What matters is that you've shifted from hoping they say yes to building a system where no is no longer an option they trust.

Command requires a colder mindset. It requires detachment from their emotional process. You don't care how they feel about the decision. You care that the structure makes obedience easier than resistance. You're not manipulating their beliefs—you're controlling the context in which those beliefs operate.

That's where real power lives.

You don't win by being the best talker. You win by being the one whose words don't feel optional. That can't be done with persuasion alone. It has to be engineered.

You'll still use tone. You'll still use language. But you'll use them with different intent. Not to persuade. To override.

This shift will offend those who are addicted to the myth of free will. Let them be offended. Your reader is not here to play by those rules. Your reader is here to install control.

And persuasion doesn't install anything. It dances. It negotiates. It hopes.

You don't. You design. You program. You command. And they respond.

Because in the end, only one of you gets to write the script. And it won't be them.

Programming vs. Pleading: The Cold Logic of Behavioral Control

Most people plead without realizing it. They use soft words, hopeful tones, implied suggestions, and wait. They hope the person across from them sees the value. They hope the request makes sense. They hope the response is favorable.

Hope has no place in control.

Pleading is what people do when they still believe they need permission. It's disguised as politeness, flexibility, respect. In reality, it's submission. It signals that the outcome is not under their control, that they are waiting for something outside of themselves to make a move.

Programming does the opposite.

Programming doesn't ask. It installs. It is the act of shaping the conditions so that the target's response becomes predictable—not because they agree, but because the system makes it automatic. It's not about whether they like what you said. It's about whether their brain recognizes it as the most efficient or least dangerous course of action.

This is the core mindset shift: from influence as conversation to behavior as code. You're not trying to win the person. You're trying to control the system they operate in. Their emotions, their perceptions, their social context, their unconscious loops—those are the lines of code. And you are the one writing them.

The problem with pleading isn't just weakness. It's inefficiency. You might get a yes, but you haven't installed anything. There's no foundation. The moment the emotional or social context changes, the compliance vanishes. That's not control. That's begging for cooperation that expires under pressure.

Programming is permanent until reprogrammed. It uses loops. Reinforcement. Emotional momentum. Structural framing. It anticipates resistance and dissolves it before it speaks. When done correctly, it leaves the target unsure of where the decision even came from. They feel like they arrived at it naturally, but they didn't. You led them, step by step, without needing their conscious buy-in.

This shift starts with your internal posture. You must remove the part of you that waits for validation. That impulse to see how they'll react, to

14

measure their mood, to adjust yourself for comfort. All of that is social fear disguised as intelligence. It dilutes your presence. It signals weakness. Programming begins the moment you stop negotiating with their emotions. Most of what makes programming effective isn't what you say. It's what you build before you speak. The silence. The posture. The priming. The context. If you walk into a room and their body already registers you as an authority, your words don't land as suggestions. They land as instructions. That's the goal.

Behavioral control isn't about intensity. It's about inevitability.

Once you stop trying to persuade, once you stop phrasing your words like you're asking for a favor, you'll notice a shift in how people receive you. They'll stop thinking. They'll start responding. The brain prefers shortcuts. Programming is the act of handing those shortcuts to people and letting them believe they found them on their own.

This doesn't require aggression. In fact, aggression often signals insecurity. Programming is colder than that. More detached. You don't command because you need them to listen. You command because the structure you've built already ensures they will.

Programming begins by controlling what the subject perceives before they make any decision. That means controlling the environment, the pacing of the conversation, the language you choose, and most of all, the emotional context. You are not reacting to their mood. You are generating it. You are designing the state from which their behavior will emerge.

A compliant subject is not compliant by nature. They are compliant because the system around them removes the friction of resistance. When resistance costs more than agreement, most people obey. Not because they were convinced. Because they were conditioned.

This is the cold logic you must internalize: people want the path of least resistance. If you construct that path in advance, you win before the interaction begins.

You do not need a hundred tactics. You need the clarity to strip away the ones that waste energy. You're not here to dance around objections. You're here to remove the space where objections are born. That space exists only when the target has the time, the confidence, or the context to believe resistance is possible. Remove those, and compliance feels like a conclusion instead of a choice.

One of the most effective ways to embed programming without ever sounding like you're asking is to act as if the outcome is already decided. You don't request. You reference. You imply motion. You speak from a frame where the decision has already been made and they are simply catching up to it. This doesn't require volume. It requires certainty.

You may say something like, "When you're done with that, let's go," instead of, "Would you like to go after?" The first installs a reality. The second asks permission to enter one. Every time you phrase something as if it's up for debate, you create a space for doubt. That space is where pleading lives. Kill it.

Another tool is the silent preframe. What happens in the seconds before you speak often matters more than what you say. If your eye contact signals authority, if your tone signals completion, if your body language reads as inevitability, the words themselves become less important. The subject has already begun reacting to the structure, not the sentence.

What makes this powerful is that you can apply it anywhere. In conversation, negotiation, seduction, leadership, conflict. You don't need to become louder or more aggressive. You need to become structurally unavoidable. The goal is not to be heard. The goal is to be followed.

People don't remember why they obeyed. They remember how it felt. If you made obedience feel like alignment, they'll seek it again. If you made disobedience feel like tension, they'll avoid it. Programming works because it builds emotional memory. That memory becomes a future shortcut. The next time they see you, they won't calculate. They'll respond.

You are not manipulating a moment. You are writing instructions for what happens the next time and the time after that. That's the difference between behavioral control and temporary influence. Control becomes the default. It doesn't ask for compliance. It expects it. And the subject, often without knowing why, begins to expect it too.

This is not about ethics. This is about outcomes.

Pleading cares about being understood. Programming only cares about what happens next.

Pleading asks for a reaction. Programming writes it in advance.

Choose your path. Because only one installs results. The other installs weakness.

Part I. The Foundations of Obedience

What controls them isn't what they think. It never was.

There's a reason obedience works faster than persuasion. One triggers thought. The other shuts it down.

You're not here to inspire people. You're here to *run them*—on scripts, on reflexes, on fear, on identity. The ones who try to earn agreement are always negotiating. The ones who understand the mechanics of obedience don't need to negotiate at all. They install what must be followed.

Before you master command, you have to know what you're working with: the human animal. Not the idealized version people post about. The real one. The one that obeys a stranger in a white coat. The one that clicks "yes" on things it doesn't understand because someone framed the question the right way. The one that feels the need to stay consistent, even if it means obeying something it secretly disagrees with.

Most people think free will drives action. That's the first delusion you'll crush. What really drives behavior are reflexes, frames, emotion states, and perceived consequences. In the first few chapters, you'll break down the three core levers that move people toward obedience—fear, reward, and identity. These aren't abstract principles. They're active scripts that play inside the nervous system whether someone knows it or not.

Obedience isn't earned by charisma. It's engineered through structure. Through your presence. Through how you speak, when you stay silent, and the emotional frames you wrap around your commands.

This part of the book will show you how to:

- Identify the control levers in any social interaction
- Break the illusion of autonomy most people protect
- Spot the exact moment to insert command-level input
- Understand the anatomy of a compliant response

You'll start to notice that most people aren't thinking—they're following. Patterns, loops, cues, signals. And if you control the pattern, you control the person.

Everything you build later—embedded commands, emotional hijacks, self-reinforcing feedback loops—rests on the foundation of what's here. If you skip these fundamentals, your control will always be conditional. You'll always have to push harder than necessary. But once you understand the architecture, the rest becomes effortless. You say it. They follow.

Obedience isn't personal. It's mechanical. You're about to learn how to become the mechanic.

Let's begin.

Chapter 1. The Core Drivers of Human Submission

Fear, Reward, and Identity: The Three Invisible Levers

There are only three reasons anyone obeys: fear, reward, or identity. Strip away the surface details, the justifications, the stories people tell themselves, and you'll always find one of these levers underneath.

These are not optional tools. They are the underlying architecture of all obedience. Every act of compliance you've ever seen—from the military to religious cults, from customer service scripts to high-level negotiations—was built on one or more of them.

If you understand how to trigger these levers, you no longer need to rely on chance. You control outcomes by controlling the emotional pressure points behind them.

Fear

Fear is the oldest lever. It is fast, direct, and reliable. People will obey to avoid pain, shame, rejection, exposure, or loss. Most don't even process it cognitively. The nervous system reacts before thought kicks in. This makes fear one of the most efficient ways to create immediate compliance.

You do not need to threaten someone directly to use fear. That's amateur work. Subtle implication is far more effective. Fear works best when it feels like it came from the subject's own anticipation, not from your demand. Your job is to suggest consequences, not enforce them. A raised eyebrow, a pause in speech, a strategic silence, or a carefully placed "are you sure that's the smart move?" can create internal collapse.

The power of fear lies in imagination. The more vividly they can project the cost of disobedience, the less resistance you will face. You don't have to force action. You let the discomfort of imagined pain drive it for you.

Fear-based obedience can be instant. But it also carries risk. If used constantly, it creates emotional fatigue, rebellion, or avoidance. It is a high-efficiency tool but must be used with precision and timing. You are not building a prison. You are building a trigger.

Reward

Reward operates on the opposite axis. Instead of threat, it promises gain. Obedience becomes the path to pleasure, approval, recognition, or access. Most people are reward-driven at the behavioral level, even if they deny it intellectually. They move toward what they believe will improve their state. The mistake manipulators often make is trying to buy compliance. That's not how true reward-based control works. You don't need to deliver the reward. You only need to imply that it exists and that it is only accessible through the behavior you want.

This is why social approval is one of the most powerful forms of reward. It doesn't need to be given directly. A compliment withheld until obedience is displayed. A positive shift in tone after agreement. A small gesture that communicates inclusion. These subtle signals activate the reward circuitry.

More important than the reward itself is the anticipation of it. Dopamine spikes before the result, not after. If you control the moment of expectation, you control the behavior. Make the target feel that they are close to winning something valuable, and they'll double down on obedience to secure it.

Identity

Identity control is the long game. It doesn't just trigger obedience. It maintains it without ongoing effort. When you alter someone's identity, you no longer need to manage their actions. They will self-regulate, not to serve you directly, but to remain consistent with the version of themselves you've shaped.

Most people think of identity as fixed. It's not. It's elastic, especially under social pressure or in emotionally charged environments. People are constantly asking themselves, "Who am I in this situation?" The answer changes depending on the signals they receive. You provide those signals.

The key is to assign identity subtly. You never say, "You are now this." You reflect it back to them. You hint at it. You reward behavior that aligns with it and ignore behavior that doesn't. You create conditions in which the only version of themselves that feels seen, respected, or safe is the one that serves your structure.

An identity can be built with something as simple as language. Say, "You're the kind of person who knows how to handle things quietly." Or, "You've always been someone who keeps your head when others lose theirs." That's not a compliment. It's a script. If accepted, it becomes a reference point. The next time they hesitate, they'll recall it—not because you pushed them, but because they don't want to violate the story you gave them.

You're not asking them to obey. You're suggesting that obedience is already part of who they are.

When used correctly, identity becomes the strongest of the three levers because it operates below the level of conscious decision-making. Someone who complies out of fear may later regret it. Someone who complies for a reward may change course if the payoff shifts. But someone who obeys to protect their identity will defend the behavior, even justify it to others, because now it represents them.

This is why cults don't need to surveil every member. They've installed identities. The system is protected from the inside. When someone believes that questioning the leader would mean betraying their higher self, compliance is no longer external. It's internal. And much harder to break.

You can use the same mechanism. You don't need robes or rituals. You only need precision in how you define, reward, and reflect back the identity you want the subject to adopt. When done with consistency, the target will not only obey—they will begin to enforce the standard themselves.

Mastering these three levers means you never have to guess again. You'll know exactly where to press and when. If someone is reactive or defensive, lead with identity to lower resistance. If someone is status-hungry or insecure, bait them with reward. If someone is unpredictable or manipulative, use fear to pin them in place. You do not need to use all three at once. But when layered together, they create a closed loop.

Fear pushes them. Reward pulls them. Identity holds them.

This is not theory. This is how institutions, relationships, governments, and corporations operate beneath the surface. They do not control people through logic. They control them through these three invisible levers. You're simply learning to do it consciously.

The difference is, you will no longer be the one being shaped. You will be the one shaping. And the people around you will never quite understand why their compliance feels so natural.

That is the point.

The Myth of Free Will: Why People Aren't as Autonomous as They Think

The average person believes they are free. They believe they think for themselves, choose for themselves, and act from independent judgment. This belief is not just wrong. It is the very illusion that allows control to work.

Free will, as most people define it, is a comforting story. It protects the ego. It makes people feel powerful, sovereign, in charge of their destiny. But beneath that narrative is a much colder reality. The mind is not a commander. It is a reaction machine, responding to internal patterns, environmental inputs, emotional states, and social conditioning—most of which operate below conscious awareness.

Every decision people make is framed by structures they did not choose. Language, culture, memory, trauma, fear, reward expectation, identity bias, social mirroring. These forces shape the boundaries of thought long before a person forms an opinion. By the time they "decide," the decision has already been influenced, if not entirely prewritten.

This isn't speculation. It's measurable. Neuroscience has shown that the brain begins preparing for a decision *before* the subject is consciously aware of making it. The mind doesn't lead. It just rationalizes what the deeper machinery already set in motion. What people call free will is usually just the conscious mind catching up to a command that was already sent.

This should not disappoint you. It should excite you.

Because if people are less autonomous than they think, that means they are more programmable than they admit. You don't need to overpower their will. You only need to understand how it's constructed. Once you see the code, you can rewrite it. Quietly. Efficiently. Without resistance.

The belief in free will is one of your greatest tools. As long as people think they are choosing, they won't question the structure around the choice. They'll fight to defend decisions they never truly made. They'll argue passionately about opinions they didn't form independently. They'll resist being controlled, even as they follow your frame, your pace, your cues, your direction.

This is why so many fail at control. They try to crush the illusion. They try to make people admit they've been manipulated. That's unnecessary. Let the subject believe they are free. It's cleaner that way. They obey faster when they think it was their own idea.

Control is not about stripping away choice. It's about defining the perimeter of what feels like choice. You don't need to dominate their decisions. You need to control what feels normal, expected, acceptable, and safe within the context you've designed. People rarely move beyond the edge of that space. Not because they can't—but because they no longer believe they want to.

The more subtle the control, the more powerful it becomes. If your influence is visible, it can be questioned. If it's internalized, it becomes indistinguishable from the subject's sense of self. That's the real prize. Not action, but internal alignment. Once that's in place, compliance is no longer an effort. It's a reflex.

One of the most effective illusions sustaining the myth of free will is the human tendency to rationalize after the fact. People rarely admit this. Instead, they build logical stories to justify choices already made by emotion, conditioning, or unconscious momentum. They believe their reasons are solid. They believe their actions reflect thought. But what they're really doing is reverse-engineering a narrative that protects their self-image.

You can use this flaw to your advantage.

When you control the input—whether emotional, environmental, or linguistic—you don't have to worry about the subject's reasoning. They'll create the reasoning for you. Once the action is taken, their brain will work overtime to make it feel congruent with their identity. If you've shaped that identity in advance, their own rationalization process will strengthen the control loop.

This is why obvious control often fails. When someone realizes they've been manipulated, they resist—not because the manipulation failed, but because the illusion of autonomy was broken too early. They react to the feeling of being forced, not to the content of the command. You can avoid this entirely by embedding your influence below the threshold of awareness. Let them rationalize the behavior. Don't interrupt it. Let the illusion hold.

Cognitive dissonance is another tool you can exploit. When someone acts in a way that conflicts with their self-image, their mind cannot tolerate the discomfort for long. They will either change their behavior or reshape their identity to match the action. If you can get them to obey just once—just enough to violate the image they previously held—they will often adjust their internal narrative to make the behavior feel natural. One act of obedience can cascade into full alignment, not because they were convinced, but because their brain needed the discomfort to stop.

This is why your goal is not to argue someone into compliance. Your goal is to insert behavior that creates dissonance, then allow the subject to resolve that tension by adjusting their self-concept. You didn't force them. You offered an action. They took it. Now they have to live with it. Most will resolve that friction by identifying with the obedience itself.

People do not resist control because they value freedom. They resist it because it threatens their illusion of authorship. If you never trigger that threat, you can control more completely. They will describe their behavior as empowered, even as it follows every cue you set in motion. They will call it instinct. Or logic. Or confidence. Let them.

When people think of control, they imagine force. They imagine domination. But the most effective control happens when no one sees it. When the subject feels autonomous, but every move is traced back to a sequence you initiated. That's not just influence. That's authored reality.

This is where the obedience algorithm becomes truly effective. You're no longer competing for attention or permission. You're no longer navigating conscious resistance. You are creating the frame that defines their options, their desires, their sense of self. The rest happens automatically.

You do not need to make people believe they are free. They already believe it. You only need to operate inside the blind spot that belief creates. That space is where commands slip in unnoticed, where structures take hold without being questioned, where your influence becomes indistinguishable from their own voice.

That is the space you control. That is where obedience lives.

The Power of Predictable Triggers in Human Behavior

Human behavior is not random. It follows patterns—loops built from fear, repetition, identity, and learned reward. Most people don't notice these loops because they're inside them. They mistake their reactions for decisions. They think they're responding to logic. But they're reacting to triggers. And those triggers are astonishingly easy to predict.

What looks like personality is often just a habitual pattern in response to familiar cues. A person raised in fear will interpret silence as danger. A person wired for approval will lean toward the strongest source of validation in the room. A person who identifies as a leader will follow commands—if they are phrased as autonomy. The surface behavior changes. The trigger remains consistent.

Predictability is power. It allows you to move before the subject does. It allows you to place cues in their environment that feel harmless but activate loops that lead exactly where you want them. Most compliance is not driven by content. It is triggered by context. A word, a look, a tone, a pause—these are not decoration. These are commands in disguise, if you know how to use them.

One of the most reliable triggers is *emotional state*. People in heightened states—stress, excitement, confusion, attraction—are more suggestible. Their cognitive filters drop. They begin reaching for shortcuts. The brain wants to conserve energy. In that moment, the first strong direction offered is usually accepted. It doesn't have to be brilliant. It has to be timed.

If you want someone to follow, don't focus on the words. Focus on the state. Shift it first. Then speak.

Another trigger is *sequencing*. If you can get someone to agree to a small action, the probability that they'll agree to a larger one increases sharply. This isn't about logic. It's about momentum. The act of saying yes creates a temporary self-image as a cooperative person. That image creates pressure to remain consistent. Consistency is a deeply programmed human need. When you violate it, the brain produces discomfort. When you reinforce it, the brain relaxes.

This is why skilled operators never ask for the big thing first. They don't trigger defense. They build sequence. They create a loop of yes. Each yes reinforces the next. By the time the subject reaches the actual command, they're already deep inside a structure they didn't notice being built.

Triggers also emerge from language itself. Some words carry implicit authority. Others carry ambiguity. Words like "because," "clearly," or "as you know" create the illusion of logic without needing to prove anything. When used early in a sentence, they set a frame. Most people don't break the frame. They move forward as if it were real.

Consider this: Ellen Langer's study at Harvard showed that people waiting to use a copy machine were significantly more likely to comply with a request when the asker gave *any* reason—even if the reason was meaningless. The phrase "because I need to make some copies" worked almost as well as "because I'm in a rush." The trigger wasn't the logic. It was the structure. The word "because" itself created the illusion of justification.

The lesson here is not about being clever. It's about being systematic. The average person is not unpredictable. They are running scripts. You don't need to decode their psychology. You only need to know which buttons activate which loops.

In high-stakes environments, predictable triggers become even more effective. The more pressure someone feels, the more they revert to instinctive patterns. Their mind narrows. Their options feel fewer. They become easier to direct, not harder. This is why crisis moments often produce blind obedience. The structure becomes more powerful than the individual.

One of the most reliable triggers under pressure is the need for *closure*. When someone is in a state of uncertainty, ambiguity becomes painful. The brain will default to the first available resolution simply to escape the discomfort of not knowing. If you position yourself as the provider of clarity, the subject will follow your lead—not because your direction is best, but because it ends the loop.

This is not about helping. It's about timing. Insert your command just before their internal pressure peaks. Frame it as the obvious next step. Do not offer options. Offer relief. They'll take it.

Another loop you can exploit is *social mirroring*. Humans constantly scan for cues about what others are doing and adjust behavior accordingly. It's ancient survival logic. When people don't know what to do, they look at the group. In a group setting, even the slightest social proof—agreement, repetition, eye contact—can activate the herd response. If you signal

26

confidence, others will defer. If you act as though compliance is already in motion, others will join. It's not manipulation. It's direction.

The trick is to trigger the pattern without alerting the conscious mind that a decision is being made. Conscious awareness is what slows obedience. Keep it unconscious, and you maintain momentum. You don't ask, "Do you want to move forward?" You say, "Let's move forward." You don't check for alignment. You act as though it's already present.

Behavioral patterns are not just exploitable. They are the default setting of most of the population. The percentage of people who make decisions with full cognitive engagement is tiny. The rest follow cues. They obey structure. They run loops that were installed during childhood, education, relationships, media consumption. And they rarely update them.

This gives you an advantage. You're not trying to convince someone to change who they are. You're using who they already are as leverage. Their fears, their need for status, their hunger for belonging, their discomfort with silence, their bias for consistency—these are tools, not obstacles.

You can also reset a trigger when it stalls. If a loop stops mid-pattern and the subject begins questioning the frame, shift their emotional state. A quick disruption of their current state can reopen the loop. Use a sharp command, a change in tone, a break in eye contact, or even a subtle disqualification. These pattern interrupts confuse the subject just long enough to reframe the moment. Then you insert the next direction. Confusion followed by clarity is a powerful form of control. They exit the moment thinking they made a decision. You know better.

Every behavior has a trigger. Every trigger can be installed. And every installed loop becomes part of the obedience structure.

This is how you make control feel like intuition. You don't force behavior. You architect the path that behavior wants to follow. You don't make people act against themselves. You create conditions where they act according to a version of themselves you defined.

There is no need to overpower people when you can out-sequence them.

This is not about being clever. It is about being precise. The operator who understands behavioral triggers does not improvise. He observes. He aligns. He places the next cue where it will be accepted automatically.

And the subject obeys, not because they are weak, but because the loop felt natural. Because the pattern matched their programming. Because you didn't fight their system. You became it.

Chapter 2. The Obedience Formula: Input → Reaction → Control

Coding the Input: What to Say, How to Frame, When to Deliver

Control isn't in what you want. It's in what they hear. The most powerful operators don't speak more clearly—they speak in codes. Their words are embedded with structure, timing, and psychological weight. It's not about talking. It's about *input design*.

Human beings don't respond to language in a raw form. They respond to *framed meaning*. That frame is built before the sentence ever lands. If you control the frame, you control the interpretation. A command wrapped in the illusion of a choice feels like freedom. A suggestion delivered in a moment of cognitive overload feels like insight. The structure of the message determines its obedience rate.

The first principle is that language is never neutral. Every word activates assumptions. The mistake amateurs make is believing that people listen to content. They don't. They scan for tone, pattern, and emotional payload. That means your words must be engineered—not improvised.

Let's start with *what to say*. Language that produces compliance is usually simple, present-tense, and framed as inevitable. "We're doing this now." "This is the next step." "You already knew this was coming." These phrases do not ask for permission. They reinforce a timeline that feels already decided. Humans avoid breaking continuity. If something *feels* like it's already in motion, they're more likely to go along.

You must remove escape routes. Words like "maybe," "try," "can you," or "I think" introduce uncertainty. Uncertainty weakens command. Use declarations, not invitations. The more direct the sentence, the more control it asserts. But directness without *frame* becomes aggression. That's why timing is critical.

When to deliver the input is often more important than what you say. An average phrase delivered during peak vulnerability can trigger deep compliance. Peak states include confusion, emotional arousal, transition between environments, moments of silence, and points of social exposure. These are not coincidences. They are pressure points in the cognitive system. When you insert the right sentence at the exact pressure point, resistance collapses. Not because it's logical—because it's easier than defending.

If you want someone to take an action, don't explain it. Precede it. Say something that implies movement is already decided. "When you get started on that..." "As you're stepping into this..." The command becomes embedded in the assumption. It skips the filter.

This is *frame-based speaking*. You build a reality in which the command is simply the natural outcome of the situation. You don't say, "Do this." You speak *from* a world where it's already been done.

That's how framing works: it creates a container for the command so the subject doesn't question the content. The brain prioritizes coherence over accuracy. It will accept flawed logic if it feels internally consistent. Your job is to create that consistency around the action you want.

We're about to move from framing into the deeper architecture of *sequence anchoring* and *command stacking*. This is where obedience stops being a hopeful outcome and becomes a repeatable process. But before we do, you must internalize one truth: timing isn't just a detail. It is the lever. Say the right thing at the wrong time and you look aggressive. Say an average thing at the perfect time and you look like leadership. What matters isn't just what enters their ears. It's what state they're in when it does.

To make the structure unbreakable, you must layer your input. This is where *command stacking* becomes essential. Rather than delivering a single instruction and waiting for a response, you pre-load multiple micro-directives that shape the subject's mental trajectory before the primary action is even introduced.

For example, instead of saying, "Go make the call," you say, "You've seen what needs to happen. That's already clear to you. The timing is right. Make the call." Each line before the final directive builds pressure and direction. You are not suggesting. You're walking the subject down a staircase where the only natural step left is the one you intended from the start.

These layers aren't accidental. Each one primes the nervous system. They answer questions the subject hasn't consciously asked. "Is it the right time?" "Is this my decision?" "What happens if I don't?" Your language must anticipate and neutralize resistance before it forms. When the internal dialogue has been answered in advance, compliance feels like self-direction. Another level of structure involves *sequence anchoring*. This is where you attach the command to a temporal or emotional anchor, so it feels inevitable. The easiest example is tying the action to an identity phrase: "As someone who handles what needs to be handled, you already know what comes next." This works not because it's true, but because it reinforces coherence. People obey most easily when the action matches the story they believe they're living. Give them a story they want to maintain—and insert the action inside it.

Sometimes the anchor is emotional. If the subject is already in a heightened state—agitated, thrilled, uncertain—you use that intensity to create velocity. "In moments like this, clarity is power. That's why you act now." Again, the command doesn't stand alone. It rides the emotional wave that's already present.

The most potent delivery happens when *nothing is left to interpret*. You remove ambiguity, not just from the words, but from the pacing, eye contact, vocal tone, and timing. The person must feel, not think. Thinking invites objection. Feeling bypasses it.

This is why hesitation is fatal. If you delay, if you qualify, if you signal uncertainty with your voice or energy, the frame cracks. You've introduced a counter-option: resistance. Once resistance appears, you've lost the simplicity of control. Every word after that becomes harder to embed. Every second of delay adds cognitive distance. You don't speak to negotiate. You speak to finalize.

The tone that works best is *inevitability*. Not aggression, not desperation. Inevitable. As if what you're saying was always going to happen and you're just naming it out loud. This creates the perception of force without the need for force. The subject feels pulled rather than pushed. That difference is the edge between success and failure in high-stakes obedience dynamics. Another tactic that strengthens control is *contextual closure*. This means ensuring the subject has no need to exit the frame you've created. You provide a beginning, middle, and implied conclusion. You speak in a way that contains their options. "You've already made the call internally. This is just the part where you execute it." The command feels like closing a loop, not opening a new one. Humans seek closure. If your input feels like resolution, they will follow just to end the tension.

Repetition without variation also increases absorption. Not repeating the same sentence, but reinforcing the core frame from multiple angles. The subconscious registers this as "certainty from multiple sources," even when all those sources are you. This mimics social proof and internal authority at once.

Everything you say, and the moment you say it, should feel like a lock clicking into place. The words are just the surface. The structure is underneath. And once that structure is installed, you no longer need their agreement. You already have their behavior.

That's what coding the input really means. Not clever language. Not persuasion. It's architecture. And when you build it correctly, they walk through the door without knowing who designed it.

Hijacking Cognitive Loops to Shape the Reaction

If you control the loop, you control the outcome. That's the central truth behind most human behavior. People don't act from pure thought. They act from loops — sequences of thoughts, sensations, reactions, and narratives that repeat beneath awareness. And unless you interrupt or redirect these loops, they will always lead to the same behavior.

The mistake manipulators often make is trying to force an action through argument or incentive. That's surface-level. What you need is *loop access* — the ability to insert your directive *within* the subject's pre-existing cycle of internal responses. When done correctly, this creates the illusion that their choice came from them, even though you built the reaction sequence that led them there.

Every loop starts with a *trigger*. This might be a question, an emotion, a change in tone, a movement. Most people are triggered by the same things every time: rejection, approval, risk, uncertainty, silence. Once the trigger fires, the subject moves into a familiar internal motion. Thoughts race. Emotions spike. The brain searches for pattern recognition. You're not here to disrupt that cycle. You're here to *take it over*.

Let's say the subject feels dismissed or uncertain. That emotion triggers a common loop: overanalysis. They ask themselves, "Why did that happen? What did they mean by that? What am I supposed to do now?" This is the entry point. You don't provide the answer — you inject *your* directive as the *resolution to their loop*. "They're just testing you. Now's the moment to show clarity." You've hijacked the narrative, closed the loop, and embedded a course of action that feels like self-generated logic.

You can also hijack loops with *micro-corrections*. These are subtle interventions delivered while the subject is mid-loop. When someone starts repeating a pattern — defensiveness, justification, doubt — you interrupt not by contradicting them, but by giving their current thought a next step that benefits you. "Yeah, and if you already know that, then you also know what needs to happen now." You don't fight the loop. You redirect its momentum.

The most effective way to gain loop access is through *predictable pattern surfacing*. Humans rarely realize how predictable they are until their loop is named out loud. When you speak the subject's internal script — especially before they do — they momentarily lose control of it. "You're probably already wondering if saying yes means giving something up." That single sentence creates a split-second of cognitive submission. They've been seen. Their loop is no longer private. And now you have room to overwrite it.

Some manipulators try to flood the loop. This is a mistake. Overwhelming the subject's thought process doesn't create compliance — it often creates freeze. You don't want freeze. You want continuation. Think of the loop like a track. You're not trying to derail the train. You're switching its destination with a hidden junction the subject doesn't see. Subtle. Silent. Precise.

In high-pressure environments, emotional loops are your best leverage. Panic, guilt, validation, revenge — these loops move fast. That means less conscious filtration and more susceptibility to external guidance. When someone is spiraling through a fast loop, your role is to *frame the resolution as obedience.* "You want peace? Good. Then fix it." You've turned their emotional goal into your behavioral command.

The key isn't in the language. It's in the sequencing. You identify the loop. You speak it before they do. You offer the next step that ends it. And that step must be the action you want them to take. Not suggested. Not implied. *Embedded.* This is the engine of internalized obedience.

The most potent loops to hijack are the ones tied to *identity.* When someone begins to question who they are — or affirm who they believe they are — they're in the most malleable state possible. Identity loops don't run on logic. They run on coherence. The human mind craves to be consistent with the story it tells about itself. If you control the input that defines that story, you control behavior at the source code level.

Let's say someone thinks of themselves as competent, sharp, respected. If you subtly imply that their compliance aligns with that identity — "Most people wouldn't get it, but I know you will" — you're not making a request. You're closing their loop in a way that *demands* a particular reaction. They comply not because they were persuaded, but because not complying would break their own self-image. That's the loop you want.

You don't need perfect timing to hijack a loop. You need pattern memory. If someone always shifts tone when challenged, if they always go silent when pressured, if they always ask for validation when unsure, then you already have the rhythm. The better you map it, the more seamless your input feels. Eventually, the subject won't even feel interrupted. They'll believe they "suddenly realized" what they had to do — unaware that realization was your design.

When building obedience at scale, preloading loops into the environment is more efficient than constant intervention. You do this through *priming*. Words, images, emotional tones — all of these can be planted early, so that when the loop begins, your desired endpoint has already been emotionally associated. For example, repeatedly reinforcing the idea that decisive people act without hesitation makes hesitation itself feel like a threat to identity. Then, when the subject hesitates, the discomfort drives them into your desired action to reassert control. That's not suggestion. That's loop engineering.

One of the easiest ways to deepen the effect is to *collapse time perception*. Most loops feel like long processes: "First I need to figure this out... then I'll act." But if you remove the space between awareness and action, you short-circuit the deliberation. Instead of guiding someone through a reflection, you convert that reflection into immediate action. "You already know what the right move is." That one line compresses cognition into obedience. It disables their internal brakes.

People think they make choices. What they really do is finish loops. If you've shaped the loop, the choice is already predetermined. It's only a matter of time. That's why patience is not the enemy of control — it's its amplifier. You can wait for the loop to begin, or you can provoke it. But once it's running, the closing move belongs to you.

If the subject tries to step out of the loop consciously, that's where you trigger the *meta-loop* — the loop about the loop. "Notice how you always stop right when it matters most?" Now their attempt to escape becomes another pattern you can name. And naming it, once again, puts it under your control. Resistance becomes routine. Routine becomes readable. And once it's readable, it's programmable.

The art is to never be seen as the source. If the subject believes the loop was self-contained, you remain invisible. That's where your power multiplies. Because once someone believes their decisions are their own, even when they're not, they stop guarding against influence. They stop checking for intrusion. They become open-source.

Every mind runs on loops. The difference between control and chaos is who closes them. Make sure it's you.

Closing the Control Cycle Before They Notice It

Obedience isn't just about initiating control. It's about closing the cycle before awareness catches up. Most people don't resist because they're strong. They resist because they notice. Your job is to remove the noticing. That means collapsing the gap between influence and internalization so that compliance feels like a natural continuation of their own thought process.

Every control sequence has a point of entry, a middle loop, and a point of closure. The point of closure is where obedience locks in. It's where the target no longer evaluates the action — they simply move forward. The longer that space remains open, the higher the risk that the subject will reflect, pull back, or seek external validation. Closing the cycle early is how you steal that space from them.

What triggers that closure? Completion. Humans crave endings. A sentence, once started, begs to be finished. A gesture, once begun, begs to be completed. Even stories we don't like, we still want to see how they end. This innate need is what makes completion triggers so dangerous. When used intentionally, they override second thoughts, silence resistance, and seal the behavioral outcome as inevitable.

One of the most effective forms of this is the *illusion of choice*. You present two options — both of which lead to the same outcome — and the moment a decision is made, the brain closes the cycle. "Would you rather handle this now or after lunch?" That line is not about the when. It's about embedding the *what* — that it *will* be handled. The cycle closes not when the action is completed, but when the mind believes the decision is owned.

Another technique is known as *false finality*. This is when you act as if the decision is already made — and the subject complies to match the emotional context. For example: "Perfect, I'll note that down for you." The action hasn't even begun, but you've spoken as if it has already been accepted. If the subject is unsure, they now have to consciously reject something that feels like it's in motion. Most won't. It's easier to go along than to stop the flow. This is how finality is created through tone, not argument.

Timing matters more than intensity. Completion triggers must occur *right* before the subject reaches reflective distance. That is, the moment before they pause to think. This window is tiny — often just seconds. But within that moment, the right phrase, signal, or assumption can cement the next step as automatic. If you miss that window, you invite evaluation. If you hit it, you embed obedience as momentum.

There's a psychological mechanism known as *preemptive anchoring*. You suggest how someone will feel after taking action before they've taken it. "You'll feel better once you've done this." This creates a mental future the subject begins to identify with. Now, to not follow through feels like a rupture in self-image. That pressure alone is often enough to seal the deal. They obey, not out of agreement, but to avoid the discomfort of dissonance. When you apply these techniques at scale, you stop needing persuasion. You shift from pushing people toward outcomes to guiding them along a preloaded track. And if that track ends just before they notice they're on it — you've already won.

The more fluid the experience, the less the subject questions it. That's why clumsy influence collapses under scrutiny, while smooth control glides in unnoticed. It's not about what's said — it's about how many gaps you leave for interpretation, reflection, or reversal. A well-placed completion trigger eliminates those gaps entirely.

Another layer of control happens through *ritualized motion*. When an action is paired with a consistent sequence — especially physical — the brain begins to associate the movement with compliance. This is why military drills are so effective. The body is conditioned to respond through form, not evaluation. You can simulate this effect even in casual environments by introducing mini-rituals: the way you hand someone a document, the phrasing you use when giving instructions, or even how you nod. When repeated consistently, these behaviors become subconscious signals that closure is occurring. People fall in line because the moment *feels* familiar.

There's also the tool of *false urgency*. While urgency is often used in persuasion to prompt action, its deeper power lies in disabling thought. "We need this locked in before the meeting." It doesn't matter whether that time constraint is real. What matters is that the subject's mind is steered away from *whether* to act and into *how fast* they must act. Once that frame is in place, the cycle closes on speed, not depth. By the time they reflect, the choice is already behind them.

This is where most so-called persuaders fail. They argue until the subject agrees. But agreement isn't closure. Action is. And action happens fastest when there's no perceived space left for decision-making. You don't need permission. You need trajectory. When the mind believes the sequence has already begun, obedience becomes easier than interruption.

Pre-loading decisions is another way to do this. You set up the subject's expectations in advance so that, when the moment comes, it feels like they're simply fulfilling something already chosen. "Once we finalize this, you'll be the first to try it." This uses future pacing to create a sense of inevitability. People don't want to contradict a version of themselves that already committed. They step forward not because they were convinced, but because they were *positioned*.

In environments where power is more diffuse — like teams or social groups — you can use *distributed closure*. This means securing micro-agreements from multiple people at different stages, so that when the final moment arrives, it feels like a consensus. No one wants to be the lone dissenter when momentum has been socially staged. One person says yes, another agrees passively, a third adds a nod. By the time you reach the fourth, the cycle feels complete. Even if it isn't. That perception alone makes opposition feel like friction — and friction, for most, isn't worth it.

The ultimate goal is to make obedience feel like completion. Not a choice. Not a compromise. Not a battle. Just the next natural step in a sequence that already had velocity. When you master this, you don't just win influence — you eliminate the need for it. Because by the time they could object, the door has already closed behind them.

Most control fails because it invites feedback. It leaves an opening. A pause. A visible mechanism. But mastery is silent. It leaves no evidence. Only results. When obedience feels like inevitability, the cycle is closed. And by then, it's too late for anyone to reverse it.

Part II. Engineering Behavior Through Language and Triggers

If Part I revealed the structure of obedience, Part II is where you learn to write the script. Control isn't abstract. It's constructed, word by word, gesture by gesture, loop by loop. The difference between someone who tries to influence and someone who commands obedience is language — not just what is said, but when, how, and with what hidden structure underneath.

Most people speak to be understood. You will learn to speak to engineer. Language, in your hands, becomes a scalpel. Every sentence becomes an insertion point. You're not asking for action. You're writing the code that makes it inevitable.

You'll start by breaking down the hidden logic behind framing — how to say the same thing three different ways and get three entirely different results. You'll learn the exact timing windows that bypass resistance, the power of delivery that softens scrutiny, and the formula for making commands sound like ideas people believe they invented themselves.

Then we'll go further. Into structure. You'll learn how to implant a trigger, set a loop, activate a sequence — and walk away. Because obedience doesn't always happen in the moment. Sometimes, the real effect detonates days later. What matters is that you built it correctly.

This part of the book gives you something persuasion will never teach you: detachment. You don't need to plead. You don't need to chase. You speak, and the world rearranges. Not because you yelled the loudest, but because you calibrated the system.

These are not tips. These are operational tools. Once installed in your way of communicating, they change how others experience you. You stop sounding like someone who wants agreement. You become the presence that frames reality for others — and they follow, even if they don't understand why.

This is the point where most manipulators plateau. They get reactions, but not results. Attention, but not authority. That's because they use language like noise — unrefined, desperate, crude. But real power is silent. It doesn't yell. It doesn't explain. It doesn't negotiate. It simply reshapes what the other person *thinks* they're choosing.

And so, you begin the real engineering now. Not just the what, but the how. Not just behavior, but the internal sequence that precedes it. This is where you stop being someone who tries to influence, and start becoming someone whose presence *writes the outcome* before anyone else has even realized what's happening.

Chapter 3. Installing Authority Without Permission

Authority Positioning: How to Be Perceived as the One They Follow

Control doesn't start when you open your mouth. It starts before you speak — in how you are perceived. The human mind doesn't decide rationally who to obey. It *senses* it. And that sensing is shaped by a combination of environmental cues, behavioral signals, and subconscious frames that communicate one thing: "This is the dominant presence in the room."

If you fail to install authority before delivering a command, you will always sound like you're asking. The framing will override the words, and your influence will feel optional. But when the frame is properly established, even vague suggestions land as instructions. Authority positioning is the subtle manipulation of perception that makes your commands feel inevitable.

Let's begin with one of the most overlooked levers: *environmental control*. People don't respond to you in a vacuum. They respond to you through the context you allow or construct around you. If you control the frame — the physical setting, the dynamics of who moves, who waits, who interrupts, who listens — you install a subconscious understanding of hierarchy before a word is spoken.

The one who commands space, commands people. Entering last, standing while others sit, not being the one to initiate greetings — these micro-acts signal non-neediness. People feel the power gap, not through aggression, but through assumed entitlement. The one who moves less, waits less, speaks slower, and occupies the center of the space is subconsciously identified as the one to follow.

But beyond the environment, the *emotional tonality* of your presence matters. Neediness, nervousness, rushed speech — these leak power. Authority is communicated by stillness. Still eyes. Calm pauses. Uninterrupted pacing. The less energy you exert to control the interaction, the more control you actually have. Your demeanor says, "This is how it's going to be," without explaining why.

This leads us to a critical behavioral hack: *assumptive interaction*. People mirror the social expectations you project. If your body, tone, and presence carry the unspoken assumption that others will comply, they often do. The moment you speak as if obedience is the natural response, it destabilizes resistance. It signals that social proof already exists, even if it doesn't.

Consider how confident leaders behave in uncertain situations. They don't ask if things are okay. They declare what's next. They don't fill silence with justification. They let silence *be* the justification. This dynamic forces others to resolve their internal ambiguity by syncing with your certainty. It's not about aggression. It's about saturation — filling the room with your chosen frame so completely that no other interpretation survives.

There's also the visual layer. Wardrobe, posture, eye contact — all part of the authority algorithm. But not in the cartoonish way self-help books portray it. You don't need a suit. You need *coherence*. Every visible signal you emit must align. If your clothes, body language, and tonality send mixed messages, the unconscious mind of your target picks up on the inconsistency. And inconsistency breeds doubt.

True authority is not what you claim. It's what others *assume* in your presence, without being told. This means the most powerful positioning comes from what you *withhold*. Excessive explanation, qualification, or emotional overexpression collapses your frame. The moment you try to prove you're in control, you've already surrendered it. Authority radiates through implication, not demonstration.

One of the strongest behavioral hacks to use here is *selective silence*. Most people fear silence and rush to fill it. Those in control, however, use silence as a weapon. When someone speaks and you don't immediately respond, you create psychological dissonance. Their brain begins working to resolve the ambiguity. Did they say something wrong? Are you unimpressed? Are you judging? That vacuum triggers internal compliance mechanisms. They adjust themselves toward your approval — without you saying a word.

Another tactic: *minimal reactive behavior*. The higher your perceived authority, the less you need to respond to emotional spikes, insults, or challenges. The person with the most social power in a room doesn't react — they *observe*. They don't need to win small battles, because the war is already settled. If someone tries to interrupt or dominate you, staying composed, pausing, and then continuing on your terms frames them as irrelevant. The crowd doesn't follow the loudest — it follows the most certain.

There's also a deeper manipulation tool built into human cognition — *pre-emptive framing*. If you speak in a way that defines what something *means* before anyone else can interpret it, you own the reality being shaped. Example: "You'll notice how quickly things fall into place when you act on this." You haven't asked them to follow you. You've assumed it will happen, and you've framed their compliance as a sign of alignment and intelligence. This bypasses resistance by removing the option of disagreement.

Even your spatial placement can be used tactically. High-authority individuals often occupy central or elevated positions, remain physically still, and use eye movement sparingly. Too much physical movement is read as nervousness or seeking approval. Control is signaled by *still dominance* — a calm, rooted presence that makes others lean toward you for validation.

Another layer of environmental hacking is control over timing. Authority doesn't rush. If you're always early, always available, always explaining, you place yourself below your target. If, instead, you show up when *you* decide, leave others waiting occasionally, or speak at a slower pace than those around you, you install the perception that others are adjusting to *your* rhythm. The one who controls the tempo, controls the dance.

In advanced dynamics, you can also weaponize *ritual*. Repeating small behaviors, symbols, or environmental elements — always drinking from the same cup, always starting meetings in the same position, always using the same pen — these create behavioral anchors that signal consistency and self-possession. Others unconsciously attach meaning and gravity to these patterns. Your rituals become part of your aura. They add layers to your persona that make people feel like they are entering *your* world, where *your* laws apply.

None of this works if you leak incongruent energy. Authority isn't just a set of tricks. It's a psychological positioning you must install in yourself first. If you are uncertain internally, it will show up in micro-signals that destroy your frame. Your belief in your own dominance must be rehearsed, embodied, and constantly reinforced — not for morality, not for authenticity, but because *belief is transmissible*. Others pick up on what you believe about yourself.

Authority positioning is not about appearing perfect. It's about appearing inevitable. Your presence doesn't need to be likable, it needs to be unchallenged. Because when the mind stops questioning *why* you're in charge, it starts asking *how to serve you best*.

Controlling the Frame: Power Is in the Setup, Not the Argument

Most people think power is about being right. It's not. Power is about controlling what *right* even means in the first place. If you're playing on someone else's field, by someone else's rules, you've already lost. True control doesn't happen in the argument. It happens before the argument even starts. It happens in the *frame*.

A frame is the invisible lens through which reality is interpreted. It defines what matters, what doesn't, what's normal, what's outrageous, what's winning, and what's losing. Whoever sets the frame defines the game. The person who can impose the frame doesn't need to win debates, because they've already shaped how the conversation is *measured*.

For example, imagine someone accuses you of being manipulative. If you accept their frame — that manipulation is wrong — you've already lost. You're defending, explaining, justifying. But if you redefine the frame and say, "Only amateurs think persuasion is accidental," you've made control sound like intelligence. Now *they're* the ones who look naive. They either step into your reality or look foolish outside of it.

This is frame control in motion. And the first rule of controlling the frame is this: *Never enter theirs*. The second you respond defensively, you've accepted the rules they set. Instead, always shift the lens. Always redefine the terms. When someone tries to put you in a box, burn the box and sell them a new one.

There are several tactical ways to control frames in real interactions. The first is *frame assumption*. You simply speak and act as if your frame is already the accepted reality. You don't argue for it. You behave *from* it. When you do this with conviction, people calibrate themselves to your certainty. Their resistance dissolves before it can activate. They begin to mirror your interpretation without realizing it.

Another is *frame flipping*. This is used when someone tries to challenge or diminish your authority. Instead of resisting, you absorb and reverse it. If someone mocks your seriousness, say, "Of course I take it seriously. That's why you're here, listening." You don't negate their challenge. You *convert* it into proof of your superiority. That's how dominant frames create rebuttal immunity — they don't block attacks; they metabolize them.

Next is *pre-framing*. This involves subtly suggesting how a situation should be interpreted *before* it unfolds. Example: "You'll probably notice how quiet people get when real influence is present." Later, when others fall silent around you, it reinforces your status as a force. You've installed the expectation in their mind. When reality matches it, they lock it in as truth.

Another technique is *absurd counterframing*. If someone challenges your logic or questions your dominance, respond with something so exaggerated it shatters the tension and flips the power dynamic. If someone says, "You can't possibly believe that," you say, "Of course not. I wrote the script for your reaction last night." It introduces dissonance and reclaims initiative. You become unpredictable, and unpredictability feels powerful because it can't be easily categorized.

Each of these techniques feeds the same core mechanism: *you define the lens*. The conversation, the situation, the emotion — all of it bends toward your version of events. And once people are inside your frame, their ability to oppose you without appearing inconsistent or irrational begins to erode. Compliance becomes easier, because it now aligns with the dominant narrative they've adopted.

Now that we've laid the groundwork for how frame control actually functions in real-world scenarios they've already stepped into your reality. And once they're inside, it becomes extremely difficult for them to climb out without appearing unstable, contradictory, or socially disoriented. The brilliance of frame control lies in this psychological lock-in. People want coherence. They want their actions, beliefs, and statements to align. If they've accepted your frame in one moment, their mind will often contort itself just to stay consistent with it later — even if it means adopting conclusions they would've previously rejected.

The framing war is not about volume. It's not about logic. It's about who gets to say *what this is*. You're not fighting facts — you're sculpting meaning. People aren't moved by truth; they're moved by *interpretation*. So the key skill isn't to be more correct. It's to make your version of reality the one that others naturally organize themselves around.

This is why great manipulators rarely argue. They *declare*. Their presence radiates certainty, not aggression. They occupy the space like they already own it, and others adjust accordingly. When you speak from the dominant frame, you don't have to justify. You don't explain. You simply *imply*. And the room absorbs it.

Even silence, when framed correctly, becomes power. If someone demands a response and you remain unmoved, they begin to question *why*. Is it confidence? Is it disdain? Is it superiority? Their uncertainty feeds your control. The absence of reaction becomes a mirror that forces them to define themselves in relation to you. And in that definition, they shrink.

But let's get precise. Frame dominance isn't a vague aura. It's built on specific behaviors. One of the most effective is environmental claiming. Wherever you are — a room, a call, a social circle — take psychological ownership. This can be done through positioning, posture, interruption patterns, or calibrated irreverence. When you treat the environment as yours, others read that as status. And once you're seen as the authority within a space, your frame becomes default.

Another key behavior is narrative injection. This is when you tell a short story or observation that contains the frame you want accepted — but you embed it in a way that feels offhand. For instance, saying, "I've noticed people usually apologize more when they sense they've disappointed someone who doesn't flinch," sends the signal that *you* don't flinch, and that apologies are the expected response. You didn't demand respect. You programmed it.

Most people try to dominate by being louder or more logical. But these tactics only work inside frames. If you've let someone else define the frame, you're locked inside their architecture. It doesn't matter how smart or persuasive you are. You're a genius in their movie. You don't control the plot. But when you own the frame, the plot bends toward you.

When conflict arises, frame warriors don't get pulled into content. They stay at the level of context. If someone accuses them of insensitivity, they don't explain how they care. They say, "When someone's grounded in their truth, softness isn't always required." They redefine the meaning of the accusation. They don't fight labels — they alter definitions.

Eventually, your goal is to make your frame invisible. It should feel so natural, so self-evident, that no one questions it. People don't argue gravity. They operate within it. That's what a perfectly calibrated frame becomes — an unseen force that everyone adjusts to without realizing they've made the shift.

And once they're fully inside your gravitational field, there's no need for persuasion. Influence becomes inevitable. They'll follow you not because they've been convinced, but because in your frame, it simply *makes sense.*

Mastering Presence: The Silent Algorithm That Overrides Resistance

Before a word is spoken, control can already be established. Presence is the unspoken signature of power — a force that bypasses intellect and sinks directly into the body of the observer. Most people think presence is charisma or confidence. It's not. It's command encoded into posture, breath, eye contact, and energy. It's what makes someone shut up when you walk in. It's what makes them lean in, hesitate, obey — without understanding why.

Presence is not learned through words. It's installed through practice. It is an algorithm running on a primal level, detected by the nervous system of others before they even realize it. You don't earn presence through what you say. You install it through what you *are*, in silence. This is why men who talk too much lose control, and why those who master their presence never need to raise their voice.

Your presence is the first layer of your control architecture. Without it, the words that follow carry no weight. With it, even your silence becomes a command.

Let's begin with the most obvious and misunderstood lever: **the body**.

Your posture is your positioning. A collapsed chest, restless hands, or twitching feet signal instability, doubt, or desperation. But when your spine is upright, chest slightly open, shoulders relaxed but firm — you signal something ancient: I am not prey. More than that, you signal: I have no threat to react to, because I am the threat. Movement must be slow, deliberate. No fidgeting. No quick turns of the head. People unconsciously mirror tempo. If you are still, their nervous system slows down. If you move with calm, they move with caution.

Your gaze is the trigger. Not the stare of tension or awkward aggression, but the locked, relaxed gaze of someone who is *already certain*. Look through, not at. Let your eyes rest on the person as if you're scanning *beyond* them. Don't blink excessively. Don't look away too quickly. When you break eye contact, do so slowly and by choice. This makes others feel seen, but not in control. They are being observed — and they know it.

Your voice must follow the same algorithm. The tone should be low, slow, and controlled. Avoid rising inflections at the end of sentences, which signal doubt or appeal. Speak as if you're narrating outcomes, not requesting permission. Short silences are not to be feared. They're tools. A well-placed pause activates discomfort in the other — and they will fill the space with compliance, explanation, or justification.

Control of space is the final silent element. Those who dominate space don't just stand in the middle of the room. They *own* the energetic tension of that space. You don't lean in to hear others. You let them lean in to you. You don't pace or shift weight restlessly. You root. When you move, it's to claim. When you stand still, it's to anchor. Even the angle of your stance matters. Standing square to someone can provoke, while slightly offsetting your angle suggests relaxed confidence and territorial ease.

These elements combine into what we call *energetic weight*. Some people feel heavy when they walk in, even if they're silent. That weight is not magic. It's the product of controlled signals. It's installable, and it's trainable — but only through repetition, not thought.

Once you control the signals your body gives off, you begin to experience something strange: people yield. They soften their tone, adjust their words, slow their movements. They instinctively lower resistance, not because they've decided to trust you, but because their nervous system *can't justify disobedience*. This isn't persuasion. It's dominance through presence. And it starts with your silence.

People will not be able to explain why they defer to you. That's the point. The architecture of presence bypasses verbal logic and taps into the oldest layers of human cognition — the same layers that decide whether to fight, flee, or submit. When your presence is calibrated, others read you as the fixed point in the room, the gravitational anchor around which everything else orbits. They feel this before they think it, and by the time they notice, their body has already responded in kind.

To begin shaping this force deliberately, you need to isolate each signal and install it through conscious drills until it becomes unconscious calibration. You cannot afford to wing it. If you leave your body language, voice tone, or gaze to chance, you leave your influence to chance. And those who operate by chance never dominate.

Start with breath. Controlled breathing isn't just for relaxation. It's the base code of your nervous system. Slow, deep, unbroken breath tells your body you are not under threat. More importantly, it signals to others that you do not *respond* to pressure — you *generate* it. Practice walking into any room and regulating your breath first, before any other movement. This reprograms your state and destabilizes theirs.

Then train your stillness. Not stiffness — stillness. The kind that comes from being fully rooted in your own authority. Choose a crowded public space. Enter it with the intent to remain still and grounded for five uninterrupted minutes. Let people move around you. Don't look away. Don't fidget. Just stand. Let the discomfort rise. Let your body want to adjust. Then override it. This is how dominance is encoded: not in words, but in your tolerance for presence under pressure.

To build your gaze, find a mirror. Hold your own eye contact for 60 seconds without shifting. Then take it into social spaces. Lock eyes with someone just a beat longer than is comfortable — not to challenge, but to anchor. You're not staring to intimidate. You're holding to control tempo. You'll notice people begin to react without knowing why: they'll talk faster, laugh nervously, explain themselves, or look away. That's your trigger. You're now inside their nervous system.

The voice comes next. Record yourself speaking about something mundane. Then lower your tone, slow your cadence, and eliminate rising inflections. Rerecord it. Compare the two. Which one sounds like a man who expects obedience? Train this pattern until your normal speaking tone carries that weight. Every pause becomes a weapon. Every word lands with precision. When you speak from this place, interruptions drop to zero.

Finally, refine your spatial command. People sense territorial dominance within seconds. When you sit, do not perch or collapse. Occupy space with stillness. When you stand, do not hover or shuffle. Ground your weight evenly and claim the physical plane beneath you. When you move, let every step be calculated. You're not rushing to a destination. You are directing a scene.

Over time, these drills install a new baseline: a presence that does not react to the environment, but rewires it. You are no longer negotiating for attention or struggling to be heard. You are operating from a different layer of control — a layer where resistance softens before it's even voiced.

Most manipulation fails because the manipulator is not believable. Their presence collapses the moment it's tested. But when presence is truly mastered, there is no test. The test dissolves before it begins. People sense the frame, feel the weight, and adjust. They don't know why, and they don't need to. They've already submitted — to something they can't name but can't ignore.

Presence is the algorithm that overrides resistance before the mind has time to build it. Install it, and obedience begins before the conversation even starts.

Chapter 4. Language as a Weapon: Covert Command Structuring

Linguistic Traps: How to Embed Commands in Casual Speech

Power doesn't always bark. Often, it whispers in the cadence of casual speech, riding the surface of harmless phrases while smuggling directives into the subconscious. This is the essence of embedded command: the art of placing an instruction inside language so normal it passes beneath resistance. While others speak to be heard, you will speak to install behavior. The key is not just in what you say, but *how* you say it. The unconscious mind doesn't interpret language based on logic. It reads rhythm, tone, and familiarity. You're not trying to convince anyone. You're bypassing their filters entirely.

To understand how this works, notice how people follow suggestions when they believe the thought came from themselves. If you tell someone directly, "You should relax," they may resist. But if you say, "Some people find it easy to relax when they sit like that," you haven't told them *to* do anything. Yet their body will often follow the implied path. The command was camouflaged inside observation.

This is your arena: casual speech with hidden structure.

Let's begin with a foundational principle. Commands embedded within longer, harmless sentences are far more likely to slip through. The human brain skims language for meaning, but it *absorbs tone* without scrutiny. A downward inflection at the end of a phrase signals certainty. If you embed a directive inside such a structure, the body registers it as stable input, not threat. For example:

"You might not notice how good it feels to follow that instinct now."

At first glance, it's vague. But read it again, focusing on *how* it lands. The directive is buried: "follow that instinct now." Everything around it is soft, plausible, dismissible. That's the trick. You don't want the conscious mind to fight back. You want it to nod, distracted.

To become fluent in this, you must train your *tonal emphasis*. The words matter less than the vocal signature. Practice saying the same sentence with different emphasis patterns. Record yourself. Rewind. Notice what feels directive versus what feels like filler. You'll start to sense where power hides in plain sight.

Another method is using **tag-alongs**: phrases that disguise control as collaboration. These are softeners that create the illusion of shared choice while anchoring the listener in a preferred response. For example:

"Just take a moment, if you like, and think about how you'd handle this next time."

The illusion is that the listener is reflecting. But the frame is already set: they *will* think about what you asked. The command is masked as an option, not a demand.

You can also manipulate *temporal frames* to limit resistance. If you say, "You can decide how to respond later," you've bought silence now. Or "You'll probably notice more clarity after we're done talking" plants an expectation that favors your influence while postponing scrutiny.

These patterns work best when spoken casually, without theatricality. If it sounds rehearsed, it breaks. But if it sounds like something they've heard a hundred times in conversation, it slides in unnoticed. That's your measure of success: not attention, but undetected penetration. You're not making speeches. You're shaping perception by tone.

Every embedded directive works better when layered inside a structure that the brain finds familiar and disarming. One of the most effective formats is the **"cause-effect loop"**. This technique installs the command as the logical result of a preceding condition. People rarely challenge what they perceive as a natural sequence. For example:

"When you start listening like this, you begin to realize how much easier it becomes to just follow through."

The embedded directive here is "follow through." It doesn't arrive alone. It's the byproduct of listening "like this," whatever that means. The vagueness allows the listener to map the suggestion onto their own behavior. That makes it feel organic. In fact, the more vague the cause, the more flexible the trigger.

Another mechanism is what might be called the **"decoy structure"**. This relies on presenting multiple benign statements to create mental rhythm, then slipping the command into the middle of the pattern. For example: "Some people think about it, others take their time, and then there are those who just decide and act before the doubt has a chance to speak."

You didn't say, "Decide and act now." You didn't have to. You used social mirroring and momentum to suggest that the third group—the fast movers—are the most natural. That's what the brain leans toward, especially when under the influence of contrast.

Precision in language isn't about clarity. It's about control. Certain verbs are more neurologically charged than others. Words like "imagine," "notice," "realize," and "begin" open internal experience loops. They don't just carry meaning. They activate sensory processing. "Imagine how it feels to move with full certainty" isn't just a phrase. It's a neural ignition. The person starts imagining, and in doing so, follows your lead.

Repetition is another tool, but it must be stealthy. If you repeat the same phrase with the same tone, it draws attention. But if you vary the phrasing while keeping the core command stable, the message implants deeper. First as a thought, then as familiarity, then as impulse. Example:

"You might feel something shift. Or maybe not just yet. But when it does, and it usually does, people just follow through naturally without thinking too much."

There's no command in capital letters, no direct demand. But the repetition of "follow through" in various forms starts to feel inevitable. Repetition makes behavior feel like it's always been there.

Voice calibration is where many fail. Without the right tone, even perfect structures collapse. Too much enthusiasm feels fake. Too little energy feels untrustworthy. You're aiming for *relaxed certainty*. Speak like someone who already expects the result. No tension. No question. Like it's already happening. A downward tone at the end of embedded commands suggests finality. A soft pause before and after gives the command space to land.

Timing is equally critical. The human brain responds most to suggestion during **micro-pauses**—those barely perceptible moments between emotional beats. After a sigh. After a statement that disorients or surprises. In the silence that follows an unexpected reframe. That's where the seed plants best. The soil is soft. The filters are quiet.

You are not aiming to be impressive. You are aiming to be inevitable. This means discarding the desire to sound "smart" and replacing it with the skill of sounding *undeniable*. Your words should not compete. They should dissolve resistance before it forms. It's not about convincing. It's about configuring.

Train this by recording three-minute monologues where you speak as if someone is already following your lead. No permission. No buildup. Just embedded structure, rhythm, and intent. Listen back. Cut what sounds like effort. Keep what sounds like certainty.

Eventually, you'll stop needing to think about commands. You'll speak, and they'll be there—wired into the syntax. That's when you've stopped performing persuasion and started becoming the environment that obedience happens in.

The Illusion of Choice: Making People Think They're Deciding

Obedience disguised as autonomy is the most stable form of control.

When people *feel* like they're deciding, they resist less, commit more, and even defend the outcome as if it were their own. The trick isn't to force choices. It's to present them in such a way that every road leads to the outcome you wanted from the beginning. The structure of the decision becomes the cage, but a cage they decorate themselves.

This is the art of **choice framing**—where the individual believes they are exercising free will, while actually moving within a pre-constructed corridor. Done properly, it dissolves resistance because there's no pressure to comply. There's just a menu. They think they're choosing what to eat, but you've designed every dish on the menu.

One of the most basic but powerful techniques is the **A or B trap**. You present two options that appear to offer genuine freedom, but both are preloaded with the outcome you want. This works best when one option is slightly more desirable and the other serves as a contrast—undesirable but plausible. For example:

"Would you rather start now while it's fresh, or circle back tomorrow when you've had time to overthink it?"

You're not asking *if* they'll act. You're framing *how*. Either way, the direction is forward. The second option subtly implies weakness or delay, making the first feel not only smart but dominant. The decision appears autonomous, but it's rigged.

Another variation is the **false neutral**: you introduce a third, "neutral" option that's technically possible but contextually unattractive. It gives the illusion of balance but exists only to nudge the subject toward your preferred choice. It often sounds like:

"We can do this efficiently right now, do it the hard way later, or just let things stay as they are and see what happens."

No one who values agency wants to "see what happens." That's surrender. So what remains is speed or struggle. Efficiency wins by default, but it was your plan all along.

Humans tend to avoid extremes. This is known as the **Goldilocks effect**—they gravitate to the middle. So if you want someone to pick option B, make option A feel overly aggressive and option C seem too weak or passive. The brain likes moderation. Use this tendency by calibrating the spectrum of choices so the target lands where you want.

Tone also matters. The way a choice is delivered can suggest what the "right" answer is without saying it directly. Subtle emphasis on one option, a pause before the second, or a look of slight concern when you mention a particular path—all of these are cues. Humans aren't just listening to your words. They're interpreting what the environment tells them is safe, approved, or desirable.

The most advanced form of choice manipulation is **pre-identification**. This involves preloading the subject's sense of identity before you even present the options. Once identity is in motion, choices become vehicles for self-expression, not logic. For example:

"People who move fast usually trust their instincts. The others tend to get stuck thinking about what they should've done."

Now when you ask, "Do you want to lock it in now or wait until later?" you're not just asking a question. You're triggering a decision about *who they are*. If they want to be the first kind of person, the path is obvious. The choice has already made itself.

Control the frame, and the answer becomes predictable. Shape the decision space, and freedom becomes theater. What matters isn't what they *choose*, but how tightly the boundaries are drawn around the illusion of freedom. True dominance is silent. It lets them speak, nod, and walk into the outcome you designed. Smiling all the way in.

People cling to the belief that choice equals freedom. It flatters their ego, reassures their sense of control, and makes them less alert to manipulation. But the more choices you offer within a rigged frame, the more the illusion deepens. You don't need to fight for control when they hand it to you willingly, grateful for the chance to "decide."

The magic lies in *constraint*. Total freedom creates anxiety. The brain prefers simplicity, clarity, and closure. When someone is overloaded with too many options, they become paralyzed. When someone is offered too few, they feel coerced. But when they're given the *right* set of options—just enough to feel free, just few enough to avoid confusion—they don't even realize the design was external.

This is how you embed direction within freedom. You don't need force. You need a funnel.

The funnel begins by **priming attention**. Most people don't decide by evaluating all options equally. They notice what you show them, and they ignore what you don't. You can spotlight one path by anchoring attention to it repeatedly—through repetition, pacing, or environment—and letting the others fade into background noise. They'll choose what's familiar, what feels present, what sits right in front of them.

Even silence becomes a weapon here. When someone hesitates, just waiting—without filling the gap—creates pressure. The longer they sit in that moment, the more they need resolution. If you've framed the choices properly, the pressure pushes them exactly where you wanted. You didn't argue. You didn't plead. You simply constructed the scene, let the silence expand, and let their discomfort do the work.

To deepen the illusion, use **feedback mirroring**. When they express interest in one option, even subtly, you affirm it. A small nod, a slight smile, a calm "yeah, that's often what sharp people go with." This signals approval without giving a command. Humans are tuned to social cues more than logic. They seek alignment. And once they sense that the decision aligns with validation or group norms, they commit harder. The seed becomes a belief.

There's also the timing of when a choice is introduced. Catch someone right after they've agreed to something small—a name, a story, a shared laugh—and they're far more likely to comply with the bigger decision. This **momentum bias** is powerful. Humans want to stay consistent with their recent actions. Use this rhythm to stack minor yeses until the real decision feels inevitable.

The final lever is **ownership transfer**. Once the subject leans toward the option you designed, treat it as if they created it. Let them narrate the reasoning. Let them connect it to their values. Ask leading questions that help them justify the choice in their own terms. You're not seeking credit. You're cementing identity. When someone owns a decision emotionally, they guard it fiercely—even if it was never really theirs.

By the time you've deployed all these layers—constraint, priming, timing, mirroring, validation, and identity—there's no resistance left. There's not even awareness. The decision feels personal, inevitable, and logical. They don't feel manipulated. They feel smart.

And this is the apex of control: when obedience doesn't feel like submission, but like sovereignty. When the leash is invisible, the walk feels like freedom. Keep this principle engraved in your mind: People will do anything to protect a choice they believe was theirs. They'll fight for it, justify it, and repeat it. Not because they were told to. But because they were *allowed* to. That's the opening. That's the lever.

And once you master the illusion of choice, you no longer chase influence. You design it.

Trigger Phrases That Collapse Resistance Instantly

There are certain phrases that bypass defenses like a key fits a lock. They don't rely on logic, they don't invite debate, and they don't trigger suspicion. They go straight into the subconscious, collapsing resistance before it has time to form. These are not slogans or sales lines. They're linguistic weapons—precisely tuned tools that override hesitation, neutralize skepticism, and create momentum toward compliance.

Their power lies in how they *pattern-match* with mental shortcuts the brain already uses. The average person doesn't dissect language carefully. They skim reality through emotional filters, tone interpretation, and associative memory. A well-placed phrase—delivered in the right tone, at the right tempo, within the right frame—feels familiar, harmless, and even reassuring. That's the trap. Once it enters smoothly, it reconfigures the interaction without resistance.

Let's begin with a foundational trigger: **"Most people don't realize…"**

This phrase is disarming because it creates a hidden pressure to *not be like most people*. It subtly positions the speaker as someone who *does* realize, which immediately elevates their authority. When you say "Most people don't realize how easy it is to make this decision once they've seen it from the right angle," the listener's subconscious is already leaning in, unwilling to be counted among the oblivious.

Notice what this avoids: you're not telling them what *they* don't know. That would create defensiveness. Instead, you make an observation about "most people," which feels like an invitation, not a threat. The implied challenge is quiet but effective. It activates curiosity and self-differentiation.

Another devastating phrase: **"You probably already noticed…"**

This one flips the dynamic. It presupposes that the listener is already perceptive. It flatters their intelligence and implants a conclusion without arguing for it. When you say "You probably already noticed how calm things get when you speak that way," the listener begins searching their memory for confirmation. This bypasses skepticism entirely, because the brain wants to prove the speaker right. It wants to preserve the illusion of already knowing. Resistance collapses because the phrase doesn't demand belief—it pretends belief already exists.

Then there's this one: **"That's exactly what someone would say if they weren't ready."**

61

Use this one when someone hesitates. It's a double-bind. If they deny it, they prove it. If they agree, they surrender. Either way, the frame tightens around them. This is especially potent when used after they express doubt or delay. You've given them a label, and now they have to choose whether to accept it or escape it. But both paths bring them closer to compliance.

There's also subtle domination in: **"Look, you're free to choose... but you already know what makes sense."**

This seems gentle. It isn't. It gives the illusion of freedom while simultaneously guiding the decision. The key is the phrase "you already know." It speaks directly to the subconscious, bypassing conscious rationalization. People want to act in alignment with what they believe they *already know*. You're not asking them to decide—you're suggesting they've already decided and just need to act on it.

And one of the sharpest tools: **"That's not even the real issue, though."**

This phrase repositions the frame mid-conversation. When someone pushes back, instead of engaging their objection, you pivot. "That's not even the real issue, though" cuts off their resistance before it expands. It signals that the objection is either old news or irrelevant. You reframe the discussion on your terms without direct confrontation.

Another high-impact phrase is: **"Let's not get distracted by that."**

It creates instant conversational dominance. You're not debating. You're controlling the direction. The phrase assumes leadership without needing justification. It breaks their train of thought and reroutes it to where you want it. You're not arguing whether their point is valid. You're declaring that it's irrelevant. This works especially well in group dynamics where you want to keep momentum on your side and prevent detours from diluting your frame.

Now consider this pattern: **"The real question isn't X... it's Y."**

This works on a structural level. People are addicted to binaries and dilemmas. When you shift the question, you don't just sound insightful. You take control of the mental terrain. Let's say someone is hesitating on a decision. Instead of engaging their doubt, you say, "The real question isn't whether you're ready. It's how fast you want to move now that you are." This removes the old framing and replaces it with your timeline, your logic, your rhythm. There's no longer an internal debate. There's just the illusion of a decision already made.

Then there's **"You don't even have to believe me—just watch what happens."**

This is lethal when used with confidence. It shifts the burden of proof to reality, not argument. It creates a sense of inevitability. It sounds like certainty backed by results. More importantly, it bypasses their need to trust you. People don't want to be sold, but they love being proven right in hindsight. This phrase gives them a risk-free emotional position: they get to observe, not commit. And in doing so, they inch closer to commitment.

A related one: **"That's exactly what someone would say right before everything changes."**

It's slippery. It sounds like a throwaway line, but it seeds expectation. You're linking their current resistance to a transformation that feels imminent. It creates a narrative tension. The subconscious loves story structure. You've positioned them right before the turning point. Now any action they take afterward can be interpreted as part of that shift—even if they don't realize it consciously.

Also potent: **"You don't have to understand it yet—just do it and you'll feel it click."**

This removes the need for intellectual agreement. It makes obedience feel like intuition. It separates thinking from action, which is a core control principle. The more you can divorce analysis from movement, the faster you can shape behavior. This phrase works because it taps into the desire to "get it right" without having to work through complexity. You're giving them permission to act without full clarity. Once they act, the mind backfills the logic later.

Use phrases like these not as isolated lines, but as embedded currents inside the larger structure of your interaction. It's not about *what* you say once. It's about *how* you layer these patterns consistently—repetition without redundancy, rhythm without monotony.

Every trigger phrase must serve a purpose: break a loop, reframe a doubt, escalate momentum, or collapse resistance. When deployed with tonal precision and impeccable timing, these sentences override default thought patterns and create new ones in real time.

Master them, and you don't have to argue. You don't even have to ask. You shape the internal dialogue of the other person until the conclusion they reach feels like their own.

And that's the real trick. Not forcing obedience. Making them carry it out with conviction. Because nothing is more obedient than someone who thinks they're free.

Chapter 5. Neuro-Locking: Making Commands Stick in the Brain

Neural Anchoring and Behavioral Imprinting

There's a reason certain smells can take you back twenty years in a second. Or why one tone of voice can either calm you or trigger rage. These reactions don't emerge from conscious thought. They're anchored deep inside your neural architecture, locked into patterns that bypass logic. This is the foundation of control through **anchoring and imprinting**—creating direct associations between stimulus and state, until your presence, your words, or your touch become embedded commands.

The nervous system runs on loops. It learns by repetition, emotion, and salience. That means if you can deliver a consistent cue while someone is in a heightened emotional state, the brain will attach that cue to the emotion like a tag. Repeat the cue later, and the emotion resurfaces—even if the context is different. This is neural anchoring. It's not persuasion. It's programming.

The key is to exploit moments when the subject is **open**—emotionally aroused, physiologically engaged, or mentally absorbed. These are imprinting windows. Whatever happens during them becomes "real" to the nervous system. And once you link a cue to that state, it becomes a shortcut to the same feeling or behavior.

For example, suppose someone just experienced a surge of pride after accomplishing something, and you make a distinct gesture at that exact moment—a slow tap of your fingers against the table. You repeat this subtly across different contexts, each time when they're proud, validated, or praised. Eventually, the gesture alone begins to evoke that state. Now you can trigger confidence, motivation, or compliance simply by tapping your fingers in that same rhythm.

But anchoring isn't just physical. It can be **verbal** or **tonal**. The phrase you say. The way you say it. The tempo of your voice. If repeated with precision in the right emotional states, these cues begin to build associative bridges. That's how you create behavioral levers.

65

Imagine using the phrase, "That's exactly it," every time someone does something that aligns with your goal. Eventually, that phrase becomes a form of psychological reward. They associate it with approval, validation, momentum. Later, when they're unsure or stalling, hearing it again pulls them forward. Their body responds before their brain catches up.

You can also use emotional imprinting to bind specific **states** to **you**. This is deeper than simple anchoring. When someone consistently feels a particular emotion in your presence—calm, excitement, safety, thrill—their brain begins to associate you with that feeling. It's not just that you *trigger* it. You become the *source* of it. That creates dependency.

If you control the input (what they feel), and you associate it with a recognizable signal (a gesture, a tone, a word), then every time you use that signal, you can replay the same internal experience. This is how Pavlov trained dogs. But it works better on humans because humans imagine they're immune.

What most people don't realize is how easily they've been trained their entire lives. School bells mean obedience. Ringtones mean urgency. Certain phrases from authority figures trigger shame, pride, or submission. You're not introducing anything foreign—you're hijacking a mechanism already running in the background.

To make anchoring truly effective, **precision** matters. It's not about randomly repeating a word or movement. It's about consistency in timing, in tone, in emotional intensity. Every input must be measured. Every anchor must be clean. If your signal is muddled or scattered, the association will weaken. The loop must be tight.

Let's break down how to craft those loops. But before that, you need to understand the one rule that determines whether an anchor sticks: **anchors only stick when paired with intensity**. The brain doesn't encode neutral moments. It encodes peaks. That's why anchoring during strong emotional highs—joy, fear, relief, embarrassment—is far more effective than during calm or passive states. If the moment is charged, it becomes memorable. If it's neutral, it gets discarded. Your job is to recognize when the internal charge spikes, then drop the anchor with surgical precision.

Timing is non-negotiable. If your cue comes before the emotional peak, it doesn't link. If it comes after, the charge has already dissipated. You need to insert your signal right **as** the nervous system floods with emotional chemicals. That's when the imprint sears. This is why great manipulators seem to move "with the moment." They aren't reacting. They're **guiding** state, then tagging it.

Let's say you want to install a state of compliance. You guide the subject into that state with tone, posture, pacing, and scenario. Once they comply—physically, verbally, or even mentally—you mirror a consistent anchor: a specific word, a subtle head tilt, a vocal inflection. Then you break the state. Later, when you want the same compliance, you reproduce the cue. The nervous system recognizes it before the conscious mind can filter it.

Over time, anchors become shortcuts. You won't need to walk them through emotional shifts. You'll simply press the trigger, and the behavior reappears. But for this to work long term, you need to vary **context** while keeping the **cue** identical. The more contexts in which the signal appears, the more robust the anchor becomes. This prevents the brain from tying it to only one environment.

What's even more potent is layering anchors. Verbal plus physical. Tonal plus spatial. A phrase paired with a gesture, delivered in the same rhythm, at the same proximity, during the same state. This creates a **multi-channel imprint**. Later, even if one element is missing, the brain still recognizes the pattern and activates the behavior.

You can also reverse-engineer this process. Observe when someone is in an intense state organically—rage, anxiety, thrill—and simply mirror a cue. Then repeat the cue later in a neutral moment and observe if the emotion resurfaces. If it does, the anchor is active. You've captured the state without ever guiding it yourself. This is how skilled operators work in real time: they don't always create emotion, they harvest it.

Behavioral imprinting goes one step further. It's not just about triggering emotion. It's about locking in **actions** tied to cues. If someone repeatedly takes a specific behavior in the presence of a certain tone, posture, or emotional environment, their brain begins to link the behavior to the trigger. Eventually, they will act **reflexively**. You no longer need to ask. You only need to cue.

This is how obedience is built. Not through logic. Through looped behavior. The subject begins to feel as if the action was their idea, when in truth, it was anchored into their motor patterns. Their physiology does the work before their conscious thought catches up. This is how rituals are formed. Habits. Addictions. Submissive reflexes.

If you want to anchor a phrase, calibrate your tone to make it **stand out**. Lower your volume slightly. Slow your tempo. Let the phrase hang in the air. Don't bury it in the middle of a sentence. Give it its own space. Repetition alone is weak without **emphasis**. It's not just what you say. It's how the body hears it.

The most manipulative anchors are the ones masked as neutral. A phrase like "You always know what to do," repeated with warm tone in high-trust moments, becomes a trigger for surrender. A touch on the shoulder delivered only in decisive moments becomes a cue to follow without question. Over time, these imprints rewire the subject's behavioral default.

If you install anchors and imprints with enough consistency and precision, your presence alone becomes a trigger. Your voice becomes a state-change mechanism. Your movements pull reactions without resistance. You're no longer persuading. You're coding responses into the nervous system and watching them execute like commands.

This is not theory. It's architecture. And once you build the structure, it runs itself.

Loop Closure: Repeating Patterns Until the Behavior Becomes Reflex

Behavior doesn't stick because it's logical. It sticks because it's familiar. The nervous system runs on loops: feedback cycles that repeat until a response becomes automatic. If you want someone to obey without hesitation, the only path is repetition. Not motivational speech. Not persuasion. **Repetition**. That's what wires behavior into the spine.

When a behavior is repeated within a consistent structure—same emotional tone, same timing, same framing—it starts bypassing conscious thought. The subject doesn't evaluate it anymore. It becomes the default. This is what real control looks like. Not a one-time influence, but a **loop so tight** the behavior runs itself.

The first thing to understand is that *open loops create resistance*. When you give a command or set an expectation and it doesn't close with a clear action or outcome, the nervous system remains alert, analyzing, doubting. But if you **close the loop**—by ending it with compliance, affirmation, or resolution— you start reinforcing obedience.

Let's say you ask a person to do something. If they do it, you immediately anchor it with approval, eye contact, a subtle phrase like "That's exactly right." Then, soon after, you ask again. They comply faster. You close it again. You do this three or four times in a tight sequence. That's a *programming loop*. Now, even if they pause, the pattern is already alive. Their body expects what comes next.

But here's the key: **tight repetition must not feel like repetition**. If it feels obvious, it triggers conscious awareness. You must loop subtly, using variations in context but not in structure. For example, you guide the subject through a series of similar actions framed as different decisions. Each choice reinforces the same underlying behavior—agreeing, following, yielding. Over time, that loop becomes the spine of how they respond to you.

Repetition doesn't have to be verbal. It can be emotional. If a subject consistently feels relief after complying with you, they begin associating you with that relief. You become a neurological shortcut: follow you, feel better. That is loop closure through emotional resolution. The deeper the feeling, the stronger the bond.

You can also use **spatial loops**. Positioning yourself in a particular way when issuing instructions—standing, leaning in, maintaining direct gaze—and repeating that same posture each time you assert control. Eventually, the body links your spatial stance with the expected behavior. Even if you don't speak, standing a certain way becomes a trigger for submission.

The most important part is to **never interrupt the loop prematurely**. If the subject resists or breaks the pattern, don't immediately shift strategies. That creates chaos. Instead, return to the last successfully completed loop and rebuild from there. Behavior is not linear. It's circular. When a loop breaks, go backward, not forward. That's how you re-establish control.

Loop closure also applies to the **end of interactions**. If you leave a conversation with ambiguity or tension, the pattern remains incomplete. The nervous system doesn't reset. But if you end with a micro-resolution—something as simple as "You handled that well" or a final directive like "We'll continue tomorrow"—you complete the cycle. The next interaction picks up where the loop left off.

The mistake amateurs make is thinking that more persuasion equals more control. It doesn't. More loops do. Repeated cycles that begin with your signal and end with their compliance. These cycles become habits. Habits become reflexes. Reflexes become identity. And once you've coded identity, you're not just controlling behavior anymore. You're **shaping who they are when they're around you**.

You don't need full agreement to begin the loop. You just need the first motion. A head nod. A slight shift forward. A "maybe." These are openings. Use them. Slide in your command, wrap it in familiarity, and repeat. Every time they follow through, even partially, you mark it—verbally, physically, emotionally. Marking is what makes the loop real.

Timing is not a detail. It is the structure. When repetition happens with a predictable cadence, the brain prepares in advance. Anticipation is not resistance. It's the first sign that the loop is integrating. You're not fighting their attention span anymore. Their body expects the next cue. That's the moment you own the cycle.

If the timing gets sloppy, the loop decays. If the intervals are inconsistent, you lose rhythm. The nervous system is wired for pattern detection, and it craves rhythm. Tight loops built on stable timing install deeper than anything spoken with brilliant logic or backed by emotional appeal. In the hierarchy of influence, rhythm beats reason every time.

You should also make use of the **stacking effect**. Each time a person completes a loop—no matter how small—it stacks on the last. A glance, a yes, a shift in posture, a breath held in silence when you enter the room. They don't reset to zero. Their system is accumulating behavioral debt. The more loops completed, the more momentum you hold. Eventually, interrupting the loop would cost them more energy than just following it. That's when obedience becomes the path of least resistance.

The real architects of influence never rush the final loop. They hold it. They allow the subject to rest in the cycle until the behavior no longer feels like a reaction—it feels like identity. "This is just who I am now." That's the ceiling of loop closure. When the subject forgets there was ever a decision. When the act of following feels native, even self-initiated.

For maximum effect, you can introduce **ritualized closure**. This means embedding a specific phrase, gesture, or action that signals the loop's end. You don't make it obvious. You use it only when the pattern has been reinforced enough to accept the ritual as part of the closing. A glance paired with a certain word. A subtle touch combined with tone drop. The moment you use it, the behavior anchors, the nervous system relaxes, and the loop resolves with finality.

This ritual becomes a silent authority symbol. Over time, the subject won't need the full loop to follow. Just the ritual trigger. It acts like a backdoor command: you skip the buildup, skip the persuasion, and go straight to execution. All because you taught their system what the ritual means without ever explaining it.

The most skilled controllers operate with quiet repetition. No theatrics. No overt domination. Just the same cycle, repeated with slight variation, reinforced at precise moments, closed with exact cues. It's invisible until it's complete. And once complete, it's nearly impossible to undo. That's because the subject doesn't feel like they were pushed. They feel like they arrived. As if this new behavior was always theirs. That's the trick. And the trap.

If you want permanence, you don't demand it. You loop it. Again and again until the behavior settles beneath language, beneath choice. At that point, you're not influencing people. You're rewriting their operating system. And they'll thank you for it.

Installing Self-Reinforcing Obedience

The most powerful form of control is the kind that maintains itself. If you have to keep pushing, you're not in control. You're managing. Real power builds systems where obedience becomes the subject's default—without external pressure, without reminders, without force. It's not enough to extract a yes. You need to build the conditions where they say yes again and again, even when you're not watching. That's the role of the self-reinforcing loop.

To design these loops, the first principle is *internal attribution*. When someone follows your lead, never make the behavior feel like it came from you. Make it feel like it came from them. This is a psychological pivot point. As soon as they start to associate the act of obedience with their own initiative, the behavior begins to self-sustain. They follow because it feels like their choice. Their thought. Their pattern. Not yours.

You install this by collapsing the space between stimulus and self-identity. After they act in accordance with your command, you don't say, "Good job." You say, "That's the kind of thing you always do." That statement shifts the behavior from isolated action into self-definition. It's no longer about this one moment. It's about who they are. And people will go to war to stay consistent with their identity.

Next comes reinforcement. But not external rewards. Not bribes. Not gold stars. Those are amateur moves. External rewards create dependency. Internal feedback builds autonomy, and autonomy perceived as obedience is the holy grail. The method is simple: build environments where following your lead gives them a short-term gain they can feel, and where deviation creates a subtle, internal discomfort.

The key is emotional tension. When they obey, relieve it. When they hesitate, amplify it. Don't do this overtly. You're not punishing. You're guiding affective states. A lowered voice when they comply. A pause and shift of gaze when they stall. A withdrawal of warmth so subtle it feels like a change in weather. You're setting the emotional barometer. The brain tracks these micro-signals constantly. Over time, they associate obedience with emotional safety. Comfort. Stability. And that association is what they'll chase, again and again, without you needing to prompt it.

If done properly, your presence becomes the axis around which their nervous system orients. When you approve, they feel a release. When you

73

disapprove—without a word—they feel the unease of misalignment. The tension doesn't come from punishment. It comes from the break in a pattern they've learned to crave.

At this stage, it becomes essential to create *continuity of context*. Self-reinforcing obedience only sustains if the behavior you want matches the environment you place them in. If you want someone to continue acting in a compliant pattern, you can't drop them back into a space that rewards rebellion or hesitation. Instead, extend your frame into everything they touch. Your language. Your routines. Your spaces. If they interact with you in a controlled context, and then re-enter an uncontrolled one, you risk fracture. But if your influence is layered across multiple contexts, then obedience becomes a default operating state, not a conditional one.

The mechanism that seals the loop is what you embed after the action is complete. Not in the moment of command, but in the quiet that follows. This is where you install a reflective confirmation—a post-behavior narrative that encodes meaning. You don't let the action disappear into nothingness. You attach a story to it. Not a dramatic one. Just enough to mark it.

"You always know exactly what needs to be done."

"I can count on you."

"You handled that like someone who gets it."

These are not compliments. They are anchors. Each one gives the subject a frame in which to place their action. When repeated, these small verbal frames accumulate into a self-concept that feeds itself. The next time a situation arises, they don't have to think. The identity takes over. The loop closes before deliberation begins.

Now, reinforce this from different angles. Not just verbal. Physical presence, spatial arrangement, emotional tone. If they obey and you step closer, that becomes a cue. If you give them eye contact only when they're aligned, that becomes a signal. The human brain builds associations without needing your permission. Every repetition makes the pattern stronger.

There's a deeper layer to this. You can accelerate reinforcement by crafting situations where obedience leads to a sense of inner superiority. When they comply, they should feel like they are the one who is ahead, who understands, who is in sync with something bigger. This is a reframe of power. You don't position their compliance as submission. You position it

74

as enlightenment. Outsiders are confused. Insiders get it. You're building a tribe of one, and they are desperate to remain a member.

The most strategic operators take it a step further. They don't just reinforce individual moments. They create a progression. Each act of obedience is not just complete in itself—it leads to the next. Like steps in a staircase that the subject is climbing without noticing. You feed them tasks that grow in complexity, each one building on the last. From small gestures to actions that require investment, commitment, sacrifice. This progression forms a compliance ladder. And once someone has climbed three or four rungs, they rarely jump off. The cost of disobedience becomes too high—not externally, but internally. They've already built too much of their identity on being aligned with your structure.

Reward should be subtle, delayed, and tied to long-term gain. Instant gratification is for amateurs. You want your subject to feel that obedience places them on a different trajectory, one that others aren't on. Make them feel chosen. Not praised. That wordless difference—between being flattered and being selected—is what creates devotion instead of dependence.

Finally, you collapse the loop entirely by removing your presence as the activator. At first, your eye contact, your tone, your posture—those were the cues. But now, the cues can be internalized. A time of day. A phrase they associate with past compliance. Even the memory of your attention. These become proxy triggers. You've implanted the architecture. It runs whether you're there or not.

What you've built is not just obedience. It's a self-reinforcing system where their behavior recycles and amplifies itself. A loop where control doesn't have to be asserted, because it has been absorbed. They walk in alignment without thinking, without questioning, without needing direction. Not because they're weak, but because the structure you installed gave them strength—on your terms.

This is the apex of influence: when the subject becomes the guardian of the very pattern that governs them. And they call it freedom.

Chapter 6. The Compliance Ladder: Small Wins to Full Submission

Why Micro-Yeses Lead to Major Obedience

Control doesn't begin with domination. It begins with consent—microscopic, almost invisible, yet strategically placed. These are the micro-yeses. The subtle nods of agreement that seem insignificant in the moment, but when stacked in sequence, form a path too narrow to turn back from.

A micro-yes isn't just verbal. It can be behavioral, environmental, or even emotional. It might look like a slight lean forward when you speak, a moment of silence after your suggestion, a glance in your direction when a decision is being made. It might be a small task completed without resistance, or a question answered before it was even fully formed. These cues are often dismissed as minor compliance. But they are the entry points. Each micro-yes creates cognitive momentum. The mind, in its drive for internal consistency, begins to pattern itself around prior behavior. When someone agrees with something small—especially if they believe it was their own choice—the probability that they'll agree with the next step increases. And the one after that. This is not persuasion. This is path construction.

You never ask for the big decision at the start. You make the yeses so small they don't trigger resistance. You build familiarity, rhythm, and low-stakes agreement. A nod. A shared assumption. A favor phrased as curiosity. You're not moving them. You're warming the machinery.

It starts with agreement around safe, universal frames. "You've probably noticed how most people never really question their routines." That's a micro-yes trigger. Not because they say "yes," but because you've placed them in a shared mental framework without requiring effort. Then you link that to the next layer. "That's why small shifts are often where the power lies." Another nod. Another frame. Another small internal alignment.

This is where sequencing becomes crucial. The micro-yeses must be ordered not just logically, but emotionally. Early yeses build rapport. Middle ones build investment. Late-stage yeses build identity. If your sequence is off—if you jump too fast from agreement to action—you snap the thread. But if you pace it right, by the time the subject reaches the real command, they won't feel like they're being commanded at all. They'll feel like they're completing something they began on their own.

This is the architecture of progressive commitment. Each step seems voluntary. Each decision feels like it confirms the last. But the real shift is that every micro-yes narrows the exit path. Options shrink. Resistance begins to contradict earlier choices. Disobedience now feels not like freedom, but like inconsistency. And humans fear being inconsistent far more than they fear being controlled.

The brilliance of this technique is that it doesn't rely on overt authority. You don't need to dominate the room. You don't need to overwhelm with presence. You just need to place the stepping stones where the path becomes obvious and forward motion feels natural. When done precisely, the subject doesn't even realize they're saying yes. They just find themselves moving forward, step by step, until the final action no longer feels like a leap. It feels like completion.

What makes a micro-yes powerful is not just its subtlety, but the emotional residue it leaves behind. Each one, if crafted properly, carries a small sense of progress. Progress is addictive. The human mind associates it with competence, alignment, and momentum. This is where you begin binding identity to the chain of consent. When a subject agrees multiple times, even in minor ways, they begin to see themselves as someone who agrees with *you*. This internal alignment becomes far harder to break than external pressure ever could.

The tool sharpens further when you integrate escalation. Each micro-yes should elevate the perceived significance of the relationship. Early on, the yeses revolve around neutral frames. But as you progress, you introduce slightly riskier, more identity-laden questions. "Do you think most people are capable of seeing through the surface of things?" Now the answer carries a weight of intelligence, of distinction. If they agree, they're not just following you—they're aligning themselves with what they believe makes them smarter, more aware, more in control. That perception becomes your leverage.

By the time the subject reaches the phase of behavioral compliance, the act itself seems inevitable. You've eliminated the friction of uncertainty. They feel consistent, competent, understood. They've accepted the early propositions. They've nodded at the framing. They've leaned into your pace. If you've sequenced everything with precision, then even a command cloaked as a suggestion lands not as an intrusion, but as a logical continuation of what has already been accepted.

The mistake most manipulators make is trying to win too quickly. They push for a large behavioral shift before the smaller agreements have fused. But when each yes has been layered intentionally, when each micro-step is acknowledged by the subject as their own movement, then resistance is no longer defiance. It's self-sabotage. You've trained them, subtly, to police themselves.

One advanced technique is to install micro-yeses into shared narratives. You don't just ask for verbal agreement. You invite them to co-author meaning. "You probably already noticed what most people miss, right?" This phrasing assumes their intelligence, presumes their insight, and gives them a subtle social reward for agreeing. When they nod or answer, it's not just you they're validating. It's their own self-image. That psychological double-bind makes disengagement unlikely. To disagree with you now would mean rejecting who they've just decided they are.

The final seal in this progression is when the subject begins to predict the next yes themselves. At this stage, the obedience is pre-loaded. They respond not to what you're saying, but to the pattern they've accepted. They finish your sentences. They act without prompting. They anticipate your needs or instructions before they're voiced. This is the apex of progressive compliance. You're not giving orders. You're being fulfilled.

But understand this: the architecture collapses if you break pacing. If you ask for something too big, too soon, or violate the internal rhythm of the interaction, the subject's awareness spikes. They may become conscious of the manipulation. They may resist not because of the request, but because the spell has been broken. So your job is not just to plan the steps. It's to manage the tempo, to read the resonance, and to refine your delivery in real time.

Major obedience doesn't need force. It needs rhythm. When your micro-yeses are invisible, intentional, and stacked with emotional intelligence, the subject becomes their own handler. And the leash? It was made from their own agreements.

Building Chains of Agreement Without Detection

Obedience doesn't begin at the command. It begins long before, in the structure of the conversation. People don't realize they're being led when it feels like they're simply *agreeing*. This is the invisible foundation of command: not dominance, but consent—manufactured subtly, layered in sequence, and designed to feel self-generated.

To build chains of agreement that bypass resistance, you must first understand the anatomy of stealth dialogue. It's not about clever lines or manipulative charm. It's about crafting *frames* within your language that remove the option of refusal without making the subject aware that choice is being taken. The goal is not to corner them. The goal is to make them lean in, unaware of how the slope has been tilted.

Start with low-friction validation. "Most people don't even notice how their habits are shaped by others." This statement does two things: it creates a shared perception ("most people"), and it flatters the subject by implication—they're *not* most people. When they nod in agreement, they're aligning not with your authority, but with their own sense of insight. You're not seen as giving them a belief. You're seen as someone who *recognizes* what they already know.

The next step is *personal alignment*. This is where you move from shared worldview to personal implication. "You strike me as someone who sees through that." This type of phrase works because it's framed as an observation, not a claim. It doesn't pressure the subject to agree. It presumes agreement in a way that feels flattering and accurate. People almost never resist what makes them feel uniquely seen.

Once the personal alignment is in place, introduce *contingent logic*. This means offering statements that sound like simple reasoning, but that subtly bind identity to behavior. For example: "People who notice those things tend to act on them. Otherwise, what's the point of seeing it, right?" The trap here is that to maintain the image of intelligence and discernment, the subject must now *act* on what's been discussed. If they don't, it contradicts the character they've just embraced. You're no longer the one pushing. You've installed a script they now feel compelled to follow.

This sequence can be escalated further through *dialogue calibration*. Keep your tone relaxed, almost casual. Speak slowly. Let your silences do the work. Silence after a framing statement acts as a mirror. It reflects their internal processing back at them. You're not asking for a decision. You're letting the logic hang in the air long enough for them to claim it as their own.

A key tool here is embedded loops—statements that reopen earlier agreements to make them feel continuous. For instance: "Like you said earlier, you can't really ignore things once you see the patterns." Even if they didn't say that word for word, they'll agree because it fits the emotional arc of the conversation. You're tying previous nods and affirmations into a single narrative line, one that naturally leads toward the next action you'll request.

By the time you arrive at a behavioral ask—whether a task, a shift in loyalty, or a spoken confirmation—you've already wrapped it inside a story they've helped construct. Refusal no longer feels like a neutral option. It would create dissonance with everything they've said, felt, and agreed with so far. That dissonance is what you use as pressure—not by applying force, but by maintaining emotional consistency.

And if you've done it right, they'll thank you for the idea. Not realizing it was never theirs to begin with.

The illusion of organic progression must remain intact. You're not stringing commands together. You're guiding a series of micro-affirmations that become indistinguishable from the subject's own thoughts. That's why language structure matters just as much as content. Use soft conditionals, implication over declaration, and phrasing that feels like observation rather than instruction.

The power of stealth escalation lies in its deniability. Not just to the subject, but to yourself. You must internalize these structures so thoroughly that you no longer need to think about deploying them. They become your native tongue. If you hesitate, overreach, or over-explain, the veil lifts, and the subject's resistance reactivates.

When shaping this kind of dialogue, maintain what could be called *emotional breathing room*. Let the subject feel just enough space between your suggestions that their brain fills in the gaps. For example: "You've probably already thought about what comes next." The moment you say that, the subject begins imagining forward motion. They start predicting action, then unconsciously aligning with it. If your next statement matches their imagined trajectory, they perceive it not as direction, but confirmation.

This works exceptionally well when layered with conversational callbacks. Referring subtly to something they said earlier—not to highlight it, but to wrap it into a larger framework you're now finishing—creates the sensation of internal cohesion. "That's probably why you mentioned that thing about not wasting time." Now that past remark feels like a precursor, not a random comment. They feel like they've been moving toward this conclusion the whole time. You're just the mirror that reflects the story.

The best obedience sequences don't feel like sequences. They feel like truths the subject has rediscovered. You install them retroactively, using conversational revision. You reframe their earlier words to fit the structure you've set. "So when you said you were tired of waiting for others to take the lead, it makes sense why this matters now." Whether they meant that or not, they will agree. Because it fits the current emotional logic. Because it flatters their narrative. Because it makes sense now.

At this stage, your role is not to add pressure but to withdraw. Pressure creates awareness. Awareness breaks the trance. Instead, stay slightly detached. Let them walk toward the outcome while you hold still. They will move to close the gap because you've designed a momentum they can't pause without consequence to their own self-image.

Subtle adjustments to pacing also reinforce this. Speak slower when nearing the critical ask, but not too slow. Let your eyes hold a bit longer, but not too intensely. Let your body become still as theirs begins to move. These small calibrations signal that the shift is occurring without making it obvious. They sense the weight of the moment, but not its manipulation.

To solidify the chain, use language that marks inevitability. Not urgency. Not control. Just inevitability. "This is just where it leads." Or, "It was always going to come to this point, right?" These phrases disarm objection by dissolving it into a broader arc. Resistance becomes irrational because the destination now feels prewritten.

You don't need loud yeses. You don't even need spoken ones. A nod, a pause, a subtle leaning forward—they're all part of the progression. And once they cross the invisible line, reinforce it with minimal acknowledgment. "Exactly." No need to explain why. Let them fill in the meaning. That's what makes it stick.

Obedience, when installed correctly, doesn't feel like surrender. It feels like alignment. Not because you convinced them, but because you let them convince themselves—with words you placed in their mouth, thoughts you slipped into their head, and choices you laid out that never felt like choices at all.

Reinforcement Loops That Make Defiance Feel Wrong

Obedience becomes permanent not when it is rewarded, but when defiance becomes emotionally expensive. If saying "yes" is the smooth path, then saying "no" must feel like stumbling into thorns. The mind naturally avoids internal conflict, so your goal is to create psychological tension around resistance, not just comfort around compliance.

At the core of this technique is the installation of emotional feedback loops that penalize disobedience without requiring confrontation. You don't need to call someone out for not doing what you want. You need to make them feel subtly off when they don't. Not punished—*misaligned*. Out of sync. Less themselves.

This works best when built into identity-based framing. People are far more resistant to violating who they believe they are than they are to disappointing someone else. If you've subtly nurtured the image of them as someone who is loyal, perceptive, consistent, or devoted, then any act of disobedience that contradicts that identity begins to erode their internal coherence.

It only takes small cues. "That's not like you." Or, "You've always been the one who steps up." These aren't accusations. They're echoes of an identity you've been feeding quietly across previous interactions. The dissonance doesn't explode in their face. It sits in the background, scratching. Until they correct themselves—not to please you, but to return to harmony with who they think they are.

Another form of reinforcement is guilt, but not the kind that is pushed directly. Imposed guilt breeds resentment. Installed guilt, however, grows from suggestion. You never tell them they've let you down. You simply reflect back what their own behavior implies.

Let them remember that you trusted them. That you opened a space they were invited into. That you held them to a standard because you believed in them. Then let silence do the work. The mind fills silence with interpretation. And in that space, most people will build their own emotional cage and lock themselves inside it.

A powerful variation is regret anchoring. Instead of framing defiance as betrayal, frame it as a missed alignment with their best self. "I don't want you to look back and realize this was the moment you stepped away from what you actually wanted." This isn't a command. It's a mirror. It makes the subject anticipate a future self who feels loss over this deviation. That future regret becomes a present motivator.

There's another layer—subtle, but potent—that uses the subject's need for consistency in social perception. Once they've complied once or twice, you begin to reference that behavior as indicative of who they are. "You've shown me that you don't hesitate when it matters." Now the choice to resist becomes not just an action, but a contradiction. A fracture in their projected pattern. They now carry the discomfort of disapproval not from you, but from the reflection they think you hold of them.

Done right, these loops are invisible. You don't shame. You don't scold. You simply let them experience the internal noise that arises when their behavior steps out of alignment with the emotional frame you've established.

This is how guilt works in nature—not as punishment, but as a recalibration signal. The body detects a break in social synchrony. It pushes the individual back toward group cohesion. Your job is to make "you" feel like the reference point for that cohesion. So that any divergence from your expectations doesn't feel like a disagreement. It feels like something *off* in them.

You don't need force when you can create psychic friction. It's far more efficient to let someone internalize the expectation than to constantly remind them of it. When they start correcting themselves on your behalf, obedience becomes self-reinforcing.

One of the most effective techniques is what could be called *identity contradiction scripting*. You let them make small choices that feel like tests of character. And when they hesitate, you don't pressure them. You observe. You allow them to interpret the meaning of their own delay. You anchor silence to disappointment, and hesitation to weakness. Then, when they choose the obedient path—even slightly—you reward it subtly with approval that feels like restoration. They didn't just act correctly. They *returned* to who they really are.

The brilliance of this loop is that it hides the manipulation inside their own self-perception. They aren't following you because you're dominant. They're following you because they now associate you with the version of themselves they feel safest being. That emotional bond—between their own ideal identity and your approving presence—is one of the most potent behavioral reinforcers you can install.

To deepen the effect, layer it over time. Every act of resistance they overcome is a thread in the net. Small moments when they almost said no but didn't. Small adjustments they made that you noticed. You don't need to reward them in the moment. It's more powerful to recall it later. "You didn't have to do that, but you did. That's why I trust you." When they hear that, they won't feel manipulated. They'll feel seen. And they'll want to protect that connection.

Regret can also be implanted preemptively. Not through pressure, but suggestion. You frame choices not as binary outcomes, but as diverging timelines. "Sometimes people don't realize how close they were to something rare." This kind of phrasing is hypnotic in its ambiguity. It makes them project forward, imagining the future moment when they look back and realize the cost of deviation. The fear isn't punishment. It's missed transformation. No one wants to be the one who walked away from their own upgrade.

Another layer of dissonance can be built into their public image. You don't have to tell others what to expect from them. You just hint. "She always comes through." "He's sharp. Sees things others don't." Now defiance doesn't just feel like letting you down. It feels like disappointing the room—violating the script that's already been written about them. Most people would rather betray themselves than be seen as inconsistent by others.

The final layer is subtle and must be used sparingly: *emotional withdrawal*. When done correctly, this isn't a punishment. It's a recalibration. You reduce your energetic presence slightly—not coldness, just a quiet reduction in warmth. The contrast creates a void. They notice what's missing. Not because you punish, but because you stop feeding the loop. And if you've done your job well, they will move to close the gap themselves.

This is the beauty of reinforcement through dissonance. You don't need to speak to it directly. You design an emotional architecture that makes disobedience feel like distortion. You make them experience the weight of being out of tune. And the only relief is returning to the path you've scripted.

The loops don't force. They don't chase. They simply *exist*—in the background, shaping behavior like gravity. And eventually, resistance isn't something you break. It's something they forget how to feel.

Part III. Psychological Pressure and Social Dominance

Power isn't given. It's taken through perception, pressure, and presence.

Up to this point, you've learned how to shape frames, plant commands, and build systems of behavioral compliance. But there's a deeper layer—one where the mind no longer simply follows because it's led. It follows because it has no space left to resist. This is where obedience hardens. Not from suggestion, but from pressure. Not from permission, but from dominance. Most people crumble not because of violence, but because of discomfort. Silence, tension, contradiction, unpredictability—these are psychological blades sharper than words. The average mind is trained to seek relief from pressure, not clarity through it. That's where your leverage begins. You don't just speak. You *imply*. You don't just confront. You *bend space*. You use discomfort as a tool to destabilize their internal compass until it aligns with yours.

Social dominance isn't about being loud, flashy, or feared. It's about being the gravitational center of any room. The one whose opinion distorts the atmosphere before it's even spoken. The one who doesn't need to demand attention, because attention has been trained to seek them out. This isn't charisma. It's constructed reality.

Psychological pressure operates on anticipation, not aggression. You learn to apply tension in small doses—uncertainty here, delay there, an unexpected shift in tone, a pause that forces interpretation. And while they're busy reading you, they stop questioning you. The longer they remain mentally reactive, the easier they are to script.

This part of the algorithm isn't about words. It's about atmosphere. You begin shaping what others feel when they're around you, and how they interpret their own behavior in your presence. You become their silent reference point. Their unspoken authority. Their invisible line of alignment. Once pressure is no longer something *you feel*, and instead becomes something *you create*, you've entered a new tier of control. In Part III, you'll learn how to destabilize resistance, weaponize ambiguity, manipulate social optics, and install your presence into the psyche of others without overt confrontation.

This is the threshold where influence turns into domination. And where obedience becomes reflexive not because they agree—but because they've forgotten how to disagree.

Chapter 7. Emotional Hijacking: Controlling State Before Command

State Control = Behavior Control

Most people assume behavior is shaped by reason, argument, or external consequence. It isn't. Behavior is a byproduct of internal *state*. The way someone feels in a given moment is a far more accurate predictor of their decisions than their values, logic, or memories. This is the core loophole in human design: you don't have to change someone's beliefs to control their behavior. You just need to control their state.

State is the internal atmosphere of a person's mind and body. It is shaped by emotions, physiological cues, rhythm, tension, expectation, attention span, and perceived safety. When someone is in a calm state, they behave calmly. When they are in a frantic state, they act without foresight. When they are in a submissive state, they comply—even against their own interests. The state *overwrites* the self-image. And that's the opening.

State is never static. It is constantly being updated by subtle environmental and interpersonal triggers. The tone of a voice, the tempo of a room, the angle of an interaction, a sudden silence. All of these shift the current running inside a person, often without their awareness. This is why dominant individuals don't argue for obedience. They *engineer* the state in which obedience feels inevitable.

To create compliance, you don't start with instruction. You start with immersion. You bring the person into a sensory and emotional space where the path you want them to take feels like the only one that makes sense. If someone feels hurried, they will default to the clearest option. If they feel seen, they will seek to preserve approval. If they feel off-balance, they will reach for the nearest structure—your structure.

There is a silent physics to this. Behavior does not emerge from the surface layer of the mind. It emerges from pressure gradients inside the emotional field. You can think of internal state like a magnetic field: it subtly guides movement, posture, tone, and even thought flow. The individual believes they are "deciding." But in reality, the direction was already tilted from the start.

This is why certain people can walk into a room and shift the behavior of everyone present without saying a word. They don't need to dominate the conversation. Their presence shifts the collective state. Suddenly, everyone else starts second-guessing their words. Their pace slows. Their language adjusts. Their filters update. The state has been hijacked before the mind caught on.

If you focus on behavior without first shifting the internal state, you're always playing catch-up. You're reacting to symptoms, not causes. The most effective form of control operates *before* decision-making has taken shape. You pre-load the behavioral track by manipulating what it *feels like* to be in the interaction. Think less "what do I want them to do?" and more "what must they feel for that to become automatic?"

A person in a specific state will almost always reach for the same type of response. If you know the state, you can predict the script. But more importantly, if you can trigger the state, you can run the script.

This is why emotionally charged environments produce such predictable outcomes. Fear compresses cognition. It makes the subject abandon nuance. Pleasure expands suggestibility. It lowers resistance to new associations. Guilt flattens defiance and draws the person toward correction. These are not abstract effects. They are levers, and when you understand their placement, you no longer have to argue or persuade. You adjust the field, and the outcome aligns itself.

The master manipulator doesn't wait for the right words. He manufactures the right *weather* inside the other's body. Tension in the chest. Heat in the face. A sudden absence of certainty. A rise of anticipation with no clear outlet. These states are not ornamental. They are functional. They erase competing directives. They reshape focus. They bypass the critical filter and replace it with hunger for direction.

If someone is in a trance state, even partially, they will not evaluate what you say through their usual lens. They will scan it through the lens of emotional congruence. "Does this feel like what I need right now?" That question, if implanted subtly enough, bypasses resistance altogether. Because now, the logic isn't challenged. The logic is irrelevant. They feel pulled toward the next step without even knowing why.

This is the fundamental shift. Most people attempt to override others through facts, demands, or force. But true obedience is not extracted by confrontation. It is *grown* from the inside out. You plant a sensation. You cultivate its direction. And when the fruit of that sensation ripens into an action, they believe it was their own. That is the highest tier of behavioral control.

Presence, timing, breath, silence, and spatial pacing are the inputs of state engineering. Each of these creates micro-adjustments in the emotional temperature of the interaction. When done correctly, they create the sensation that *you* are the regulating force. You become the stabilizing frame they unconsciously rely on. Once that trust is encoded, obedience follows without prompting. You no longer need to sell the direction. You *are* the direction.

This can be done without theatrics. It is quiet. Precision over volume. Influence that feels like relief. You provide the exit from discomfort you created—or amplified—or simply allowed to become conscious. And that exit is whatever behavior you had planned for them all along.

None of this requires mystical skill. It requires attention. Attunement. Emotional calibration. You do not speak *to* the mind. You speak *through* the environment of the mind. The tone of your voice becomes more important than its content. The rhythm of your words becomes a carrier wave. The spacing of your phrases creates an opening. And the way you pause tells the nervous system what to expect.

If you can trigger the nervous system into a receptive or compliant mode, the rest is mechanical. The behavior that emerges next will *match* the shape of the state. Resistance is a state. So is submission. So is loyalty. These are not abstract concepts. They are repeatable, trainable, programmable modes of operation.

Most people live in reaction. They wait for state to come to them. But the manipulator curates state. He doesn't wait for the wind. He controls the climate. Once you can do that, it doesn't matter what they think. It only matters how they feel—because how they feel *is* what they'll do next.

This is the foundation. From here, the practical tools take form. But their power only exists because the terrain has already been shaped. Everything that follows is built on this law: control the state, and the behavior obeys. Every time.

How to Shift Emotion to Trigger Compliance

Emotions are not barriers to influence—they are the gateway. Logic filters information. Emotion moves behavior. If you want compliance, don't argue their beliefs. Shift their emotional state.

Every emotional state carries with it a behavioral predisposition. Fear seeks safety. Guilt seeks redemption. Curiosity seeks resolution. Trust seeks direction. If you shift the emotion, the behavioral impulse will follow. This is the unspoken key that obedience systems exploit. The mistake most manipulators make is trying to push commands into a resistant state. But you never push obedience. You *prime* it.

The human nervous system constantly scans the environment to decide how it should feel. It is listening for tone, looking for pacing, detecting subtle facial tension, tracking shifts in breath. When you walk into a room, you are not only observed—you are *absorbed*. You are setting the emotional field. The question is: are you doing it by accident, or by precision?

The first tool is your voice. It is more than sound—it is signal. A calm, downward-inflecting voice immediately installs a perception of authority. Fast, high-pitched speech creates anxiety or weakness. Whispered tones bring the listener inward. Broken cadence creates tension. Long, deliberate silences paired with sustained eye contact flood the nervous system with anticipation. That anticipation becomes emotional heat. And emotional heat wants release. You decide the outlet.

When your tone evokes emotional movement, the listener's logical resistance loosens. If someone is defensive, you do not counter with data. You downshift your voice. You elongate your pauses. You let them stew in the absence of pressure. You make silence louder than resistance. And when they feel the space crack, you deliver a statement—not a question, not a pitch—a statement that resolves what they didn't know they were waiting to hear.

Pacing is the next layer. Verbal speed isn't just about clarity. It sets the nervous rhythm. When you speak quickly, the listener reacts. When you slow down, they entrain. Speaking too slowly, however, can signal uncertainty unless it's paired with tension. Tension is the invisible hook. A deliberate pause just before a key phrase increases emotional gravity. People lean in when you're about to drop something—but only if the pattern suggests weight is coming. That suggestion is established by earlier cues: tone, word choice, breath control.

Emotional priming works best when it's layered. Start with neutral conversation. Set a rhythmic pace. Begin to lean into suggestive tonal shifts. Let your facial expression mirror intensity but stay contained. The goal is to create an impression of restrained emotional force. This imbalance—emotional containment in you, slight escalation in them—draws the nervous system toward calibration. They begin to sync. That sync is the beginning of psychological alignment.

Suggestion operates underneath content. The words you use are secondary to the emotional code they carry. "You probably haven't realized yet…" triggers introspection. "Some people notice this just before…" activates anticipation. "It makes sense you'd want to…" generates preemptive permission. These aren't commands. They are doorways. They move the subject without resistance because they never *asked* for anything. They simply shaped what now feels inevitable.

To trigger compliance, your goal isn't to make them agree—it's to make them feel like something just clicked. Like what you said *felt right*. That feeling of internal click is emotional momentum. And emotional momentum, once triggered, overrides doubt.

Now that the foundations of tone, pacing, and subtle suggestion are in place, the next layer is emotional saturation. This is where the subject doesn't just hear you. They *feel themselves reacting* to you, and begin to yield without understanding why.

When the emotional state becomes saturated—when the person feels tension, curiosity, safety, or approval radiating from you—their body begins responding before the mind catches up. This is when the priming becomes automatic. And once the body responds, the behavior is halfway there. The trick is not to rush. You don't yank them emotionally. You wrap them slowly. Emotion is a spiral, not a switch.

Control begins to cement the moment you let them feel *relieved* in your presence. If their nervous system associates you with the reduction of uncertainty, you gain compliance without ever needing confrontation. Your tone doesn't have to be aggressive. It has to resolve a felt need. For some, that need is clarity. For others, it's confidence. For many, it's permission to let go of control. Learn to identify what flavor of emotional saturation they seek, and become the source of it.

The more subtle the shift, the more permanent the effect. Emotional force applied obviously invites awareness, and with awareness comes defense. But when you let the emotion arrive from within them—just guided, not imposed—the change becomes self-owned. They will defend the compliance as their own decision. You will not have to justify your influence because they'll do it for you.

You don't need to be overt to be effective. Sometimes, just slowing your breath while someone speaks pulls their nervous system into sync. Their voice drops. Their tension eases. Their pace softens. In that shared rhythm, you insert calibrated inflections: tone dips, upward lures, slight smiles, narrowed eyes. These gestures register in milliseconds. They don't need to be conscious to be obeyed. In fact, the less conscious, the more binding.

If you want someone to feel guilt, you don't tell them they should feel guilty. You make them notice the contrast between who they think they are and what they've done. The same applies to any emotional state. If you want to elicit regret, you guide them into awareness of a loss they didn't realize they caused. You drop a line like, "Most people don't see what they're doing until it's already passed them by." Then you hold the silence. The silence does more than words. It forces the nervous system to react. That reaction is the emotional break. You've just created space for guilt to bloom.

Emotionally charged language has weight when it's used sparingly. If everything is dramatic, nothing is. That's why calibrated restraint is more powerful than theatrical intensity. Speak like you're barely containing something real. That's what draws people in. They want to feel what you're holding back. They lean closer. They lower their guard to receive. And what they receive is not just your words—it's the state they were designed to enter.

To reinforce the shift, you must match their emotional reactions in real time. If they soften, you affirm subtly. If they look down, you hold space. If they try to deflect with a joke, you stay silent. Don't reward disassociation. Reward immersion. The more they stay inside the feeling, the more anchored it becomes. Eventually, they will associate the experience of that emotion with your presence, your tone, your pacing. That is emotional conditioning in action.

Once the emotional state is reliably triggered, introduce micro-suggestions. These are not overt commands. They are phrases that feel like echoes of their own internal voice. "That's exactly how you should feel." "You're finally seeing it clearly." "This makes everything easier, doesn't it." Each line functions as a behavioral lubricant. It slides into the cracks of emotion and locks in the new shape. The suggestion confirms the emotion and steers its interpretation. That is the moment influence becomes durable.

You are no longer pushing. You are not even persuading. You are shaping how they interpret their own sensations. The moment someone starts interpreting their own emotional state in alignment with your intention, the body and mind unify under your direction. They stop analyzing. They start acting.

This is why skilled manipulators don't sound manipulative. They sound *correct*. Not logically correct—*emotionally inevitable*. You want the subject to feel that not agreeing with you would feel unnatural. Not because you argued, but because the emotional tone now demands congruence. And disobedience would break that tone.

That is when they surrender. Not to the force of your words. But to the shape of the feeling you sculpted around them. Once you control the emotional field, behavior falls into line. It has no choice. The compliance becomes reflex. And you remain the one who knows how to trigger it again, whenever needed.

The Fastest Paths Into Fear, Guilt, or Gratitude

Some states cut deeper than others. Fear, guilt, and gratitude are not casual moods. They rewire attention, dismantle resistance, and alter the subject's internal compass. If your goal is behavioral control, these are your levers. They bypass argument and rationality. They create internal pressure that demands resolution. And you become the resolution.

But you don't get there by accident. You use structured entry points. Emotional states like these respond to three triggers: contrast, personal implication, and unexpected intimacy.

Let's start with **fear**. The fastest way to invoke it is to remove perceived safety while maintaining ambiguity. Fear does not arise from certainty. It arises from *what-if*. Your goal is not to deliver threats. That's amateur. Your goal is to invite them to complete the threat *themselves*.

You say:

"You ever notice how fast things change when you stop paying attention for just a second?"

Then hold silence.

Let them feel the drop.

You don't finish the thought.

You let their nervous system fill in the consequence.

If their eyes shift, if their breath shallows, you follow with:

"I'm just saying… the things you think are secure might not be."

It's not what you say. It's the spacing. The drop in vocal tone. The pause that follows. Fear blooms in absence, not in noise.

Fear also pairs well with suggestion-by-implication. You imply an unknown risk by speaking in vague certainty:

"People who ignore this always regret it. Always."

Never explain. Never name the outcome. The lack of specificity activates imagination. Imagination does more damage than direct command.

Now move to **guilt**. The access point here is contrast between identity and behavior. If someone sees themselves as kind, show them their unkindness. If they see themselves as reliable, show them their neglect. The key is not confrontation. It's quiet reflection.

Say something like:

"That doesn't sound like you."

Or:

"I really thought you were the kind of person who would've noticed."

You're not accusing. You're inviting *cognitive dissonance*. That gap between self-perception and action is unbearable. They'll want to close it—and the easiest way is to align with you.

Body language is critical here. Look down, not up. Slow your voice just slightly. Let it feel like disappointment, not anger. You're not forcing guilt. You're *allowing* it.

Now for **gratitude**. This one is often misunderstood. It's not about being nice. It's about making someone feel seen in a moment when they didn't expect it. That's what creates emotional drop. The tactic here is *earned reflection*—not flattery, but acknowledgment tied to something personal they forgot you noticed.

Say:

"You didn't have to do what you did that day. Most people wouldn't have. But you did."

Then stop. Let it land.

The best gratitude triggers are retrospective. You remind them of something they've already done that had an emotional cost. But you frame it as rare. That rarity creates value. That value returns to you.

Another:

"That one time you stayed after even though you had your own stuff going on... that didn't go unnoticed."

You use their memory to build emotional leverage. Gratitude is powerful because it creates debt. Not financial, but *identity-based*. When someone feels you've *understood* them more than others do, they want to stay in that light. They want to remain worthy of your perception. That's where compliance is born.

What makes these techniques potent is not the wording alone. It's the timing, the emotional tone, and the tension between what's said and what's *left unsaid*. The space between phrases does the heavy lifting.

When used precisely, these emotional triggers do not feel like manipulation. They feel like a moment of internal confrontation. That's why they work. The person obeying doesn't think they were controlled. They think they *came to their senses.* And that illusion of self-direction is what allows you to pull the strings without resistance.

You can't afford to be clumsy with delivery. Every element of your presence must be aligned with the emotion you're invoking. To induce fear, you must sound like something is off but never say what. Slow your pacing slightly. Let your words hang just long enough for the silence to start breathing. Do not blink too often. Keep your body still except for one controlled gesture—perhaps a turn of the head, a deliberate shift in eye contact. The less movement you make, the more they project meaning into your stillness. To induce guilt, shift into reflective softness. Speak a little slower, but not lazily. Lower your volume without flattening your tone. Don't accuse. Use past-tense observations. "You usually…" or "It's not like you to…" sets the stage. The body should express quiet containment—like you're holding back something more powerful. A gentle sigh at the right moment can cut deeper than shouting.

To install gratitude, remove all excess energy. Gratitude doesn't land when it feels like strategy. It lands when it feels unprepared. Look them in the eye, then look away just before you speak. As if something overcame you. That broken eye contact creates a flash of intimacy that makes the following words land with more weight. Be quiet. Be simple. Do not try to sound wise. Try to sound honest. Say one sentence, then stop talking. Let the quiet do the rest.

If you want these emotional shifts to lead into action, close with an *open invitation that aligns with the feeling you've just activated.* That is the gateway.

After fear, say:

"I just want to make sure you're not the one who has to find out the hard way."

After guilt:

"That's not you. You still have time to make this right."

After gratitude:

"I never forgot that. I trust you'll do the same now."

These phrases are not about information. They're about momentum. You are taking the emotion you've installed and giving it a direction to move toward. That direction is always aligned with your control.

You can also layer these states for more intensity. Fear followed by guilt collapses defense and invites submission. Guilt followed by gratitude induces a redemption arc that gives them a reason to comply. Gratitude followed by fear creates a betrayal avoidance loop—they obey to preserve your perception of them.

Be warned: this only works when your own emotional expression is calibrated to the moment. People don't obey because you deliver the right words. They obey because you *become* the context in which obedience feels inevitable.

They feel the shift. They feel your calm while they're unsteady. And in that moment, what you suggest doesn't feel like a request. It feels like a lifeline. They take it without resistance, not to please you, but to stabilize themselves.

That's the power of emotional precision. It doesn't just get people to listen. It makes them *want* to align. Not out of logic. Not out of duty. But because not doing so would feel like a betrayal of something they can't quite name— only feel.

You're not aiming for rational agreement. You're shaping emotional architecture. One carefully chosen phrase, backed by the right tone and timing, can disarm the mind and rewire behavior. Once someone has felt that kind of internal shift in your presence, you become a fixed reference point in their nervous system.

From then on, your influence requires less effort. They've already felt what it's like to be recalibrated by you. And somewhere in them, they want to feel that again.

Chapter 8. Weaponizing Silence, Tension, and Discomfort

The Psychological Cost of Silence

Silence is one of the most underestimated psychological weapons. People are conditioned to avoid it. In conversation, silence feels like failure. In negotiations, it feels like threat. In relationships, it feels like rejection. You're not just pausing sound when you use silence—you're injecting pressure directly into the nervous system of the other person.

This is why those who know how to wield silence don't need to raise their voice. They don't need long explanations or endless persuasion. They know that silence makes people squirm, over-explain, confess, or submit. Because in most people, silence creates internal discomfort so severe that they will do anything to fill it—even if that means giving you exactly what you want. The trick is not just to stay quiet, but to modulate your pacing before and after the silence to guide its meaning. Silence, in isolation, is just absence. Silence placed between sharp, precise sentences becomes loaded with tension. It becomes a tool that keeps the other person locked in your rhythm.

Here's how that works in practice. Start with a clear, short directive: "You know what needs to happen." Then stop speaking. Hold eye contact. Don't blink too much. Don't smile. Don't fidget. The person in front of you will often fill the space within seconds. They will offer explanations, excuses, justifications. Let them speak. When they finish, remain silent again. That second silence cuts deeper. Now they're no longer just reacting to your authority—they're reacting to their own discomfort.

This creates an emotional spiral. Each time they speak and you remain silent, they begin to question themselves more. And each time you withhold a verbal response, you maintain power. The longer you withhold your reaction, the more they orient themselves around earning it. This is obedience without demand. Submission without command.

Silence also works exceptionally well in high-stakes persuasion. If you've just dropped a heavy truth, a directive, or a threat, do not dilute its power by continuing to talk. Say what you need to say, then shut your mouth. Let the silence do what your words cannot: sink in. People don't process commands in real time. They process the emotional weight of those commands in the pauses that follow. If you keep talking, you short-circuit that process. If you stop, you give it space to take root.

Another variation is using silence to feign disappointment or confusion, especially after someone has failed to comply. Instead of confronting them verbally, you look at them—direct, slightly puzzled—and you just wait. Don't shift your weight. Don't help them out of the moment. Let the tension rise. Let them feel your judgment in your stillness. Most people cannot tolerate being watched in silence. They will apologize. They will correct. They will try to make it right.

This only works, however, if your silence is clean. It must not feel passive-aggressive or insecure. It must feel intentional. That means you need to be fully comfortable in it. Most people aren't. Most people break their own silence too soon, chasing the other person's reaction. That collapses the effect. To master silence, you must learn to feel nothing while the other person begins to unravel.

The more emotionally volatile the person, the faster they will crack under silence. But even the calm ones will begin to sense that they're no longer in control. And that's what this is really about: silence reorders the hierarchy. Without you having to move a muscle. Without you needing to justify your position. Without needing to fight or force anything. Just by refusing to release the pressure.

You're not just withholding words. You're denying emotional closure. That's why silence works. People crave resolution. They want to know where they stand. They need feedback to orient their behavior. When you remove that feedback, they get trapped in an emotional loop, scanning your every microexpression for approval, correction, or threat. It becomes unbearable. That's when they begin to submit not to your authority, but to their own emotional tension—and you become the one who can release it, or not.

To intensify the effect, use controlled breathing and micro-calibrated body language. A slightly raised eyebrow can signal disapproval. A long, slow exhale can signal disappointment. A brief glance away can suggest you've lost interest. These non-verbal cues carry meaning that words could never hold without dilution. The silence amplifies them. It's the absence that makes presence feel heavier.

Timing is everything. Silence too early and it falls flat. Silence too late and it feels weak. The most powerful moments are when you create a rhythm of speech that builds up tension, then drop into a silence that holds it in place. You must feel the emotional energy in the room and stop precisely when it peaks. That's when the mind is most open to internal suggestion. That's when your lack of words echoes louder than any argument.

You can also use silence to trigger confession. After asking a question, say nothing. Don't nod. Don't lean in. Let the question hang, suspended in the space between you. Most people will answer. Then they'll feel like the answer wasn't enough. So they'll add something. Then something else. Eventually, they'll reveal more than they intended—not because you asked again, but because the silence pressured them to justify themselves. This is how you extract information, test guilt, or weaken resistance without appearing aggressive.

In obedience dynamics, silence is a recalibration tool. If someone begins to challenge your authority or resist your suggestions, stop engaging. Not angrily. Not dismissively. Just go quiet. Let them speak. Let them spill their energy into a space that isn't offering friction. When their wave of defiance collapses from lack of resistance, reenter with a calm, clear statement. The contrast between their emotional output and your stillness reframes the power dynamic. They look chaotic. You look unshaken. That contrast reestablishes control.

A useful exercise is to practice micro-pauses within your regular speech. Drop in silences not only between sentences but between emotionally charged words. This changes how each word lands. It forces the listener to hang on to the next phrase. You're teaching their nervous system to expect the rhythm you set. Once that pattern is internalized, your silences become commands in themselves. They no longer wait for your words. They wait for your permission.

In a group setting, silence can fracture alliances. When one person speaks against you and you meet them with silence, the others begin to feel the shift. They sense tension. They start to wonder who you're really watching, whose loyalty you'll reward, or punish. The silence becomes a selective weapon—it isolates the dissenter without confrontation. You haven't condemned them, but you've also refused to rescue them. That space becomes a void others rush to avoid.

All of this works because silence isn't passive. It's pressure. It magnifies the weight of every micro-cue, every hesitation, every breath. It turns the conversation inward. The other person starts to hear their own voice louder than yours, and that's where control lives—not in what you say, but in what they start to think between your words. If you master this space, you won't need to dominate conversations. You'll only need to pause. And watch them break their own patterns to fill what you've left unsaid.

How Tension Forces Movement Toward You

Tension is one of the most misunderstood forces in human interaction. Most people avoid it. They equate it with conflict, discomfort, awkwardness. But those who understand control know tension is leverage. It is directional energy. When used correctly, it makes people lean in—psychologically, emotionally, even physically—without realizing they're doing it.

You don't always need a clear command to gain compliance. Sometimes, you just need to make staying still unbearable. That's what tension does. It pushes the subject out of equilibrium, making them look for the easiest way to regain balance. If you've positioned yourself as the resolution to that imbalance, their movement—verbal, emotional, behavioral—will bend toward you automatically. Not because they chose to. But because you left no psychologically comfortable alternative.

There are two main forms of tension creation: **physical** and **verbal**. Both affect the nervous system in similar ways. One triggers the body directly. The other does so through language and tone. When used together, they create a multi-layered field of pressure that the subject cannot easily escape.

Let's start with physical tension. You don't need to yell or crowd someone to generate discomfort. Sometimes, the most subtle adjustments send the strongest signals. Holding eye contact slightly longer than usual without blinking. Standing at an angle that invades their peripheral awareness but not their direct line of sight. Letting silence stretch while keeping your posture completely still. These cues override social autopilot. The brain starts to scan for safety. It doesn't find it. That's when control begins to shift.

There's also the use of **micro-movements**. A slight lean forward, followed by complete stillness. A deliberate pause in your step as you pass someone. These things register subconsciously. They say: *Something is about to happen.* That creates uncertainty. And uncertainty is uncomfortable. People will do almost anything to escape it—including agreeing with you, yielding space, or modifying their tone. You haven't demanded anything. You've just created a gap they want to close.

Now verbal tension. This is where your words act like tripwires. You introduce friction into the conversation through timing, tone, and layered implication. You don't have to be aggressive. In fact, subtle challenges wrapped in politeness are far more effective. Saying something like, *"You sure you're ready for that?"* places a question inside their self-image. Now they feel watched. Evaluated. Judged. Most will move to close the gap by proving they are ready—which means doing exactly what you've implied they should.

Another tactic is controlled tempo disruption. Speak slowly, then suddenly quicken your pace. Or speak in clipped, sharp phrases when the conversation was smooth just moments before. The nervous system reacts. It senses a mismatch. People will instinctively mirror your energy to stabilize the interaction, even if that means stepping into your emotional rhythm without noticing they've done it. That's movement. That's entry.

Stacking tension works even better. If you combine physical proximity with tonal sharpness and emotional ambiguity, you create a triangular pressure field. The subject starts to lean in, not because they want closeness, but because the discomfort of distance is growing heavier. They think they're solving the discomfort on their own, but you engineered it.

Sometimes, what you *don't* say becomes the trigger. A pause that follows a challenging statement leaves them suspended. You've implied disapproval, but haven't confirmed it. That makes the mind race. They'll seek your validation to stop the inner spin. And that movement—psychological and emotional—is an entry point for deeper control.

When silence lingers right after a subtle verbal challenge, it becomes a mirror. The subject projects their own insecurities into the gap you've created. They begin explaining themselves, overjustifying, apologizing, seeking reassurance. The moment they do that, they've shifted into a submissive position. You haven't raised your voice. You haven't even moved. You've simply made the absence of your validation louder than their resistance.

Tension also affects **group dynamics**. In a room with multiple people, the one who generates the most subtle but undeniable tension often becomes the gravitational center. People orient toward them—visually, energetically, conversationally. That person becomes the perceived authority. Why? Because everyone else unconsciously tries to regulate the imbalance they're emitting. Even if no one speaks about it, the group starts moving around their emotional temperature. If you can master tension, you don't need to fight for the spotlight. The room shapes itself around you.

But tension alone is not enough. You must know when to **release** it. Think of tension as a bowstring. Keep it taut too long, and it loses its function. But when released at the right moment, it launches a result that couldn't be achieved otherwise. After you've built enough pressure, offer a small release. A shift in eye contact. A half-smile. A single confirming phrase like, *"That's what I wanted to hear."* The subject's nervous system floods with relief. That relief becomes associated with your approval. Now they seek that feeling again. They want to *earn* the release. This is how obedience becomes self-reinforcing.

The body will betray a subject's threshold. Watch for micro-reactions: a tightening of the jaw, a glance away, a shift in breathing. These are signs that tension has started to work beneath their conscious awareness. They might deny it verbally, but their physiology is showing you the truth. This is the window. If you press gently but precisely at that point—through a question, a step forward, a pause that lets them sit with what you've just implied—you'll find they move toward compliance almost reflexively. Not to please you. To escape the internal squeeze.

Your goal is not to threaten. Threats create confrontation, and confrontation breaks frames. Tension, when correctly applied, bypasses confrontation. It bypasses logic. It works beneath the surface, interrupting automatic behaviors and replacing them with your lead. That's the art. Make the air heavier, then offer yourself as the way to breathe.

Sometimes, the best application of tension is in withholding comfort that the subject is used to receiving. If someone expects warmth, withdraw it. If they expect softness in your tone, sharpen it. The dissonance alone will create confusion. Confusion breeds instability. And instability triggers the desire for correction. You offer that correction as reward for alignment. You don't request it. You allow them to reach for it on their own.

Dominance doesn't scream. It doesn't perform. True dominance is quiet control over nervous system thresholds. It's the ability to shape the space around you so that others adjust themselves to fit. When you master tension, you stop chasing influence. You start becoming the source of it. They move toward you not because they want to, but because staying where they are has become unbearable.

By mastering how to modulate discomfort—physically, vocally, and emotionally—you build an invisible mechanism of behavioral gravity. They lean in. They follow. They adapt. Not because of what you said, but because of what they felt in the space between your words. That is obedience by design. That is control without force. And that is what turns tension into power.

Turning Discomfort Into Obedience Pressure

Discomfort is one of the most powerful levers of behavioral control. People are wired to avoid tension, unease, and emotional friction. The trick is not to punish. It is to create a situation where obedience *feels like the natural relief from that discomfort.* You don't command. You engineer a state where compliance is the most comfortable option. That is the essence of turning discomfort into pressure.

Discomfort can be emotional, social, or physiological. Emotional discomfort arises when internal expectations conflict with external reality. Social discomfort emerges when the subject feels out of sync with the group or with you. Physiological discomfort arises when subtle bodily cues—pace, space, silence—trigger unease. All three can be calibrated to make obedience feel like the simplest, most natural path.

The first step is **diagnosis**. Observe carefully. Look for micro-signals: a pause too long, a flicker of the eyes, a subtle tightening of the jaw. These are the early indicators of tension. They tell you where the discomfort is brewing. Once detected, the key is to allow it to grow just enough to motivate movement without triggering resistance. Too little, and nothing happens. Too much, and you provoke defensiveness.

Next comes **framing the relief**. Once discomfort is present, you position obedience as the way out. This can be verbal or non-verbal. A simple phrase, carefully delivered, can shift perception: "It's easier if you handle it this way." Or, "You'll feel better once this is done." The words themselves are secondary. Their impact comes from timing, tone, and delivery. They must arrive at the precise point when discomfort is strongest. That moment is the pivot. Obedience then becomes not a request, but the instinctive action to restore equilibrium.

Body language amplifies this effect. Open posture, slight forward lean, controlled eye contact, and calm breathing communicate that following your lead will relieve the tension. Conversely, subtle stillness or silence when the subject hesitates increases internal friction. They feel the gap. They feel the choice. Compliance then becomes the path of least resistance, not because you demanded it, but because their own nervous system is seeking closure.

Pacing and rhythm also matter. Introduce pauses before the suggestion, letting the tension build. Speak the suggestion slowly, with slight emphasis on key words that signal opportunity for relief. Then return to silence. Let the subject internally process. This micro-cycle creates a sense that they are arriving at the solution on their own. They obey not to satisfy you, but to resolve their own unease.

Another element is **anticipation of relief**. Before giving the subject the option to comply, subtly indicate that relief exists, but do not provide it immediately. That gap generates pressure. It leverages the mind's natural inclination to resolve tension. When the option finally presents itself—whether a simple instruction, a subtle cue, or a slight nod—obedience feels immediate and rewarding. They perceive it as their choice, when in fact you created the trajectory.

Social context can reinforce this effect. If others are present, the subject's discomfort intensifies when misalignment is visible. Use micro-acknowledgments to signal approval when they move toward obedience. That approval becomes another vector of relief. The subject learns that moving toward you not only reduces internal tension but also restores social harmony. Compliance is now psychologically reinforced on multiple levels.

Finally, **consistency matters**. Every time obedience brings relief, you strengthen the neural pattern. Repetition creates expectation. The subject begins to anticipate discomfort in scenarios where you are absent, imagining that obedience will resolve it. Over time, this makes compliance reflexive, as they have internalized the relief association. Obedience is no longer an external demand. It is a self-selected pathway toward comfort.

Once the subject begins to associate obedience with relief, you can escalate the effect through **layered tension**. Introduce a small uncertainty, pause, and let them sense that the path forward is momentarily unclear. Then offer the option to comply. Each cycle of tension followed by relief reinforces the link between your direction and emotional resolution. Over repeated interactions, this pattern becomes anticipatory. The subject begins moving toward your desired outcome before you even signal it. They obey because resisting would prolong their own discomfort.

Subtle **variations in pacing** deepen the association. Quick bursts of speech or rapid gestures introduce micro-surprises, which heighten attention and arousal. Slow, deliberate phrases that follow immediately afterward provide contrast, allowing the nervous system to relax into obedience. The contrast between the moment of unease and the moment of clarity magnifies the perception of relief. You are effectively training their internal feedback loop: tension arises, obedience resolves it, and they internalize the experience as natural.

Non-verbal reinforcement strengthens these cycles. Slight nods, micro-smiles, and controlled eye contact act as invisible rewards, signaling approval without overt acknowledgment. If the subject hesitates, a subtle head tilt or calm exhale communicates that compliance will restore equilibrium. Your body language provides a continuous, low-key cue that frames obedience as the easiest, safest, and most comfortable choice. Resistance becomes internally costly, not because of you, but because their own system flags it as dissonant.

You can further intensify pressure through **strategic delays**. When you give the subject an instruction, pause before confirming it, or hold back a promised outcome momentarily. That delay introduces a small but perceivable friction. The subject will unconsciously seek to close the gap by following your guidance. By controlling timing, you amplify the perceived value of compliance. Every second of pause reinforces the idea that obedience is the pathway to resolution.

It is essential to **escalate in calibrated steps**. Begin with minor discomforts and small, simple actions that resolve naturally. Once the subject experiences the pattern, gradually increase the stakes or the complexity of the action required. Their nervous system has learned the rhythm: tension appears, compliance resolves it. The emotional expectation now favors following your lead automatically, and higher-level actions feel just as natural as the first micro-compliance.

The power of this method also lies in **self-reinforcement**. The more they comply to relieve discomfort, the more they internalize the relief as self-generated. They don't perceive it as you controlling them. They perceive it as them choosing the most comfortable action. You've shifted the locus of agency inward. Obedience becomes self-reinforcing, durable, and resistant to later questioning because it is tied to an internal sense of stability.

Finally, integrate **social and contextual cues** to compound effectiveness. If others are present, the subject's awareness of perceived observation or social alignment subtly enhances the need to relieve tension. If the subject believes compliance restores harmony or maintains status, obedience becomes a dual-layer reward: internal emotional relief and external social validation. Both layers work together to solidify the pattern.

Repeated cycles of discomfort and relief, when combined with calibrated verbal and non-verbal cues, create a **psychological architecture of obedience**. The subject moves toward you not out of fear, guilt, or gratitude alone, but because the internal cost of resisting becomes tangible. Compliance is no longer a demand; it is a path of least resistance, the automatic choice of a nervous system trained to seek balance, comfort, and resolution.

Once mastered, this technique allows you to **guide behavior subtly yet powerfully**. You do not push. You do not pressure overtly. You simply engineer the emotional landscape so that movement toward your intention feels inevitable, natural, and self-directed. Obedience becomes relief, and relief becomes habitual.

Chapter 9. The Obedience Frame in Social Settings

Group Dynamics and Social Proof as Compliance Tools

If you want fast, durable compliance without the need for constant exertion, stop targeting individuals in isolation. Start using the invisible pressure that arises in groups. Human beings don't just respond to authority or logic. They respond to context. And in a group, the context is amplified. People look to others to decide what's acceptable, what's normal, and—most importantly—what's safe. This creates a predictable, manipulable pattern: once a few comply, the rest follow.

This is not about persuasion. It's about pressure by perception. The subject doesn't need to be convinced; they need to feel seen by others who are already moving in the direction you want. That visibility acts as a mirror and a trap. Once someone sees that others are complying, staying outside the line becomes psychologically and socially uncomfortable.

There's a reason high-control systems, from military boot camps to cults, use collective behaviors. Chants, rituals, uniform movements, even synchronized breathing—these aren't aesthetic choices. They erode individuality and make compliance contagious. You're not trying to dominate one mind. You're building a controlled environment where deviation feels like exposure.

To do this effectively, you must position the group as a container for acceptable behavior. Make examples of micro-compliance public. Let others see when someone gives you a small yes, even if it's trivial. Praise, eye contact, subtle acknowledgment—these become social signals. Each small act reinforces the norm: obedience is recognized, approved, expected. Disobedience becomes increasingly awkward, even if you say nothing.

One of the most potent tools here is staged compliance. In settings where multiple people are present, pre-seed the interaction with someone who agrees with you early. This doesn't need to be dramatic. It can be as simple as a nod, a spoken confirmation, or following an instruction quickly. The others will unconsciously begin calibrating their reactions based on that initial response. If the first subject complies without hesitation, the rest are more likely to follow. If the first person hesitates or resists, it creates a micro-cascade of resistance. Your control over the first impression controls the tone for the rest.

Silence in a group also becomes a lever. If you ask for a response and no one moves, the silence grows heavy. The moment someone breaks it with compliance, everyone else exhales and follows. But you can reverse this, too. Delay your instruction, let the group build anticipation, and drop a clear command. The first mover becomes your accelerant. You only need one spark.

This isn't theory. It's neurobiological. The human brain uses mirror neurons to interpret others' behaviors as cues for its own. Seeing someone nod, agree, or act creates a shadow impression in the observer's own mind. That's why group laughter feels contagious. It's not just emotional. It's neurological mimicry. When you orchestrate group dynamics, you're engineering that mimicry to serve you.

You don't need to overtly dominate the group. You just need to direct the patterns. Guide where eyes go, who speaks first, and how others react. If someone hesitates, let the group pressure handle it. Social compliance takes over where direct authority might provoke resistance. This is why many leaders don't bark commands—they structure moments.

Now, you begin to see how power multiplies. Not because of what you say, but because of what others do when you say it. That is the architecture of influence. And once you control it, the group polices itself. You just create the conditions. They enforce the obedience.

When the group becomes your tool, resistance collapses faster and cleaner than it would under one-on-one pressure. The subject isn't just weighing your authority—they're tracking how much they're deviating from what others accept. That deviation creates discomfort. Not because of punishment, but because of exposure. The need to blend in, to not stand out as the odd one, kicks in automatically.

This is why social proof isn't about argument. It's about atmosphere. The more the environment suggests that compliance is already the norm, the less energy you need to enforce it. You just need to *frame the moment*. Use language that implies prior agreement. Phrases like "as we've already agreed," "since we're all aligned," or "everyone's ready" don't ask for agreement—they imply it already exists. Now the subject has two choices: follow along, or challenge the entire perceived consensus. Most won't risk that, especially when others are present.

Social obedience also thrives under limited ambiguity. When people aren't sure of what to do, they default to watching others. So the first to act sets the code. This is why strategic planting of actors, allies, or even brief setups in dialogue can radically swing compliance. The person doesn't feel pushed. They feel like they're falling into what's already accepted. That's the illusion you must craft.

More power emerges when you make that illusion self-reinforcing. Once someone has obeyed publicly, their identity becomes linked to that action. People want to appear consistent in front of peers. If they say yes once in front of others, they're more likely to say yes again just to protect their image. The group becomes a mirror that traps them in a loop of escalating agreement. Not because you forced them, but because they don't want to lose face.

You can accelerate this by engineering visibility. Don't allow obedience to go unnoticed. Even subtle reactions—eye contact, nods, acknowledgment—signal to the rest of the group that someone just did the "right" thing. The message is simple: compliance gets recognition. The inverse is also true. Let disobedience fall into awkward silence. Don't attack it. Don't confront it. Just let it land flat. That emptiness will do more to correct behavior than confrontation ever could. No one wants to be the one who gets the wrong kind of attention.

There's a deeper lever, too: reputational risk. In group settings, people fear being judged even more than being wrong. Use this. Build moments where agreement feels safe, easy, and applauded—while disagreement feels like it exposes them to scrutiny. You don't have to say it out loud. Just ask a question, let everyone see the responses, and pause on the one who resists. Even the act of lingering in silence after someone hesitates is enough to make them feel out of sync. That discomfort alone pushes them back into alignment.

Peer-based control outlasts direct commands because it continues after you leave. If you structure the group norms correctly, the others begin correcting outliers automatically. The system enforces itself. This is how you create authority without lifting a finger. The group does the work for you.

Your job isn't to force alignment. It's to choreograph it. Engineer the environment so that compliance looks natural, expected, already in motion. People don't want to feel manipulated, but they desperately want to be safe. And safety, in the context of a group, is defined by proximity to the majority. Make that majority obedient, and the rest will follow without needing to understand why. They'll simply fall into place, believing it was their own choice.

That's the art of invisible control. And once mastered, it allows you to command without ever appearing to do so.

Neutralizing Alphas and Dominating Social Hierarchies

In any group, hierarchy isn't just present—it's enforced. And when someone else occupies the top of that invisible structure, your influence is capped. You can't lead if another figure is commanding attention, steering perception, or controlling the social temperature. That person is the alpha. And if your goal is obedience and influence, they must be neutralized.

But removal is rarely the optimal play. Overt attacks trigger resistance. They make you appear insecure, reactive, or threatened. Worse, they spotlight the target and reinforce their social power. The smarter approach is disruption without declaration. You don't challenge them directly. You discredit, reposition, or bypass them while the group barely notices what you've done. Start with contrast. Alphas often command space through certainty, presence, and attention-grabbing behaviors. Instead of copying them, invert them. Be calm when they're loud. Be still when they move. Be surgical when they generalize. This creates friction between their energy and yours—and the group begins to feel the difference. You signal control without ever competing. Over time, others start to see their behavior as erratic, performative, or insecure. That's the beginning of the erosion.

You can escalate this with subtle status violations. Interrupt them—once—with a calm question. Correct a detail they misstate. Add precision to something they gloss over. The goal isn't to dominate them. The goal is to signal that they're fallible in front of others. People watch closely for these shifts. When you become the one who sharpens or clarifies, you become the one others defer to for judgment. Bit by bit, they start recalibrating the hierarchy.

If the group is already bonded to the alpha, repositioning works better than discrediting. Instead of trying to pull them down, recast their role. Frame them as the muscle, not the mind. The actor, not the strategist. Give them compliments that restrict their domain of influence. "You're the energy that keeps this thing moving," you might say. Or "he's the guy who gets things done, I just handle the structure." Everyone hears the praise, but what sticks is the frame: *you* are the one with vision. You reassign status without needing conflict.

A third route is bypass. You don't touch their status directly—you just render it irrelevant. This works especially well when the alpha's influence comes from social or emotional dominance rather than competence.

Introduce information, skill, or resources that only you possess. Solve a problem the alpha can't. Answer the question no one else can. The group now sees you as necessary. The alpha might still hold their posture, but their dominance loses weight. You've shifted the gravitational pull toward yourself.

None of this works if you telegraph neediness. Power doesn't beg for recognition. It asserts itself by ignoring lesser games. Your presence must radiate unbothered control. Even when you correct, reposition, or override, it has to feel inevitable—not strategic. If people detect that you're trying to climb, they'll defend the current hierarchy. But if they feel like you're simply the natural center of gravity, they'll reorganize around you without resistance.

At this point, you've weakened the alpha's grip without war. You haven't taken the crown. You've made others realize it no longer fits them.

The moment you've cracked the perception of the alpha, every gesture becomes louder. When you nod, others lean in. When you pause, they wait. When you dismiss something casually, it starts to seem irrelevant to everyone else too. Influence stops being something you push and becomes something that pulls. That's what real social gravity looks like. But to maintain it, you have to manage one final layer: containment.

A toppled alpha might not go quietly. If their ego or identity is deeply rooted in dominance, they'll feel the shift before they can name it. Expect resistance. It won't be direct—it will come in the form of passive challenges, sarcasm, performative confidence, or indirect attacks on your credibility. This is where most people lose their lead. They bite the bait. They try to reassert dominance through conflict. And the moment that happens, the group's attention returns to the old game: a contest of ego. You must not play.

Containment means you handle aggression with disproportionate calm. When they jab, you ignore. When they test, you under-respond. When they escalate, you stay completely unaffected. The contrast becomes overwhelming. They look like a child trying to provoke a wall. And when they run out of ways to bait you, their power implodes. Not because you fought harder. Because you refused to acknowledge their frame at all.

Sometimes, though, containment needs escalation. When the threat becomes too disruptive to ignore, you don't react—you redefine. You say the thing nobody else has the courage to say. You frame their behavior not as threatening, but as insecure. You point out the performance behind their dominance. You expose the need beneath the posturing. This move should be rare, precise, and devastating. It's a surgical dismantling of the role they've been playing, and if you do it right, it doesn't feel like an attack. It feels like truth.

The final layer of domination is reinforcement. Once the social hierarchy has shifted, you must stabilize it. You do this by anchoring new perceptions. Subtly reward people when they defer to you. Include others in decision-making only when it flows through you. Guide conversations in ways that center your values, your direction, your language. Over time, the group reorganizes itself around your presence. The old alpha fades from relevance, not because you destroyed them, but because you restructured the room.

This entire process must be invisible. If anyone feels manipulated, you lose. If it looks like you're trying to win, you've already lost. The power in social dominance lies in naturalization—making others believe it was always meant to be this way. That's why the best domination doesn't involve force. It involves erosion, misdirection, and inevitability.

There's no need to announce yourself. The room will know. There's no need to compete. The competition will dissolve. True hierarchy control doesn't require elevation. It requires disappearance—of threats, of tension, of any alternative authority but your own. And once that silence takes hold, people will follow you not because they're forced to. But because there's simply no one else to follow.

Triggering Obedience in Public Without Losing Status

Triggering obedience in public is a high-risk, high-reward game. Every eye on you amplifies both power and vulnerability. Ask too directly, and you look needy. Push too hard, and you look insecure. But when you trigger action subtly, without overt dominance, you project a level of control that radiates status. The key lies in embedding commands inside normal behavior—without ever looking like you're issuing one.

This is where microcommands come into play. A microcommand is not a formal request or an order. It's a suggestion wrapped inside an assumption, often delivered through tone, gesture, or timing. You don't ask someone to move—you walk as if they already will. You don't tell them to hand you something—you extend your hand at the right moment and continue your sentence. The more natural it looks, the more obedient they become. And the less they notice it.

These microcommands work because they bypass the conscious filter that looks for power plays. They don't trigger resistance because they don't feel like tests. And yet, every time someone complies, your status rises. You've become the person around whom others adjust—without ever needing to negotiate it.

One of the most effective formats is the **presumed future command**. Instead of saying, "Can you bring me the report?", you say, "When you bring the report, I'll take a look at it." It implies the action has already been decided. There's no room for refusal, but no trace of force either. You're not challenging their autonomy—you're reframing their role as already supportive.

This method can be layered with environmental cues. For example, if you're sitting and they're standing, look toward the chair beside you just before speaking. The visual cue plants a seed. When you say something like, "So while you sit here, I want to show you something," the command rides inside a completely benign sentence. But by the time they realize what happened, they're already seated—and they feel no resistance.

In social dynamics, hierarchy is rarely about volume or force. It's about who sets the rhythm. Microcommands let you set that rhythm invisibly. You lead by adjusting the tempo, the transitions, and the implied choreography of the interaction. The person being led won't notice. But everyone else watching will feel it.

Where most people fail is by trying to make their commands visible. They over-assert. They try to "look like the leader." But in group environments, overt control often triggers social suspicion. Nobody likes the person who needs to prove they're in charge. The one who commands without seeming to command, however, triggers curiosity, respect, and compliance all at once.

This is why indirect displays are equally important. Obedience doesn't always come from direct engagement. It often comes from what others see you tolerate, what they see you ignore, and what they see you elicit without effort. For instance, when someone moves to accommodate you before you ask, it creates a ripple through the group. They internalize a narrative: "He didn't even need to say anything." That perception reinforces your leverage without you lifting a finger.

In public, silence can sometimes be more commanding than words. A delayed glance. A pause before responding. A slow pivot of the body that implies disinterest. These all shape the behavior of others more effectively than overt control tactics. It's not about giving commands. It's about making people adjust to you before they realize they're doing it.

That's where status is built—not through control, but through invisible influence. Through the ability to bend behavior around your presence without force or friction.

You begin to shape reality by anchoring your identity as the one to respond to—not react to. The group watches not just what you say, but what others do around you. If people adjust their posture when you speak, if they lean in or quiet down, that tells the group who the gravitational center is. Social creatures don't measure dominance by words. They measure it by how the environment bends.

This is why your restraint becomes a weapon. The less you chase reactions, the more potent your presence becomes. People expect dominance to look aggressive. But inverting that expectation makes you dangerous in silence. A well-timed look, a casual remark wrapped in ambiguity, or even the refusal to clarify a comment—all of these techniques create pressure without noise. Microcommands rely on subtle congruence. If your voice, body, and energy all telegraph certainty, you won't need to speak in declarations. A lowered tone and a slower pace make people lean in. A still body in contrast to their fidgeting makes you feel anchored. You create a dissonance in tempo, and they recalibrate to match you. That recalibration is obedience disguised as rapport.

You also install patterns. If you consistently use short commands disguised as cues—"You'll stand here," "You'll wait a second," "Let's move"—without pause, explanation, or tension, people begin to follow reflexively. Each successful compliance becomes an unconscious agreement: "When he speaks, I act." Repetition makes it automatic. That's how influence scales inside group settings. What began as a single adjustment becomes collective compliance.

This is especially effective when paired with **social echo**. If one person follows your microcommand, others will mirror that behavior. Humans follow the first mover. You don't need to command five people. You guide one, and let the others copy out of instinct. Every visible compliance you earn is a future obedience you don't have to ask for. It becomes a visual precedent. People internalize the pattern: "This is how people respond to him."

Even subtle acts like initiating movement—walking without checking if the group follows—create a gravitational pull. Most people wait for consensus before moving. The one who doesn't creates psychological authority. It's not about leaving people behind. It's about training them to trail without being asked. When others scramble to catch up, it rewires their sense of your importance.

To preserve status while triggering obedience, you must also resist correcting people directly in public. Reframe, not reprimand. If someone resists a subtle instruction, adjust your frame so that their resistance looks like part of your design. For example, if someone doesn't sit where you gestured, you might say, "Perfect—standing will make this faster anyway." You don't lose control. You shift the narrative. In public, you never reveal friction.

You also avoid seeking acknowledgment. Needing affirmation poisons dominance. When someone complies with a microcommand, you don't thank them or smile in approval. You allow the moment to pass as if nothing noteworthy occurred. That nonchalance rewires the act as standard behavior around you, not a favor they offered. The more natural the obedience feels, the deeper it embeds.

Mastery of this form of control lies not in spectacle, but in invisibility. You become the hidden current beneath group behavior. They feel your influence without identifying its source. That's what protects your status. Overt control can be challenged. Subtle orchestration cannot. People obey what they cannot name.

You don't dominate by towering over the group. You dominate by becoming the hidden rhythm they fall into. They'll adjust their speech, their body language, even their beliefs—just to stay in harmony with your presence. And they'll think it was their idea.

Chapter 10. Controlling Romantic and Sexual Power Games

How Obedience Plays Out in Attraction

Attraction is rarely about symmetry, logic, or compatibility. It's about tension. Unequal roles, the dance between control and surrender, the invisible hierarchy that determines who orbits whom. At its most primal level, attraction is a recognition of power—emotional, physical, social, or psychological. And obedience is one of the deepest markers of that power. When someone changes their behavior to match yours, even slightly, they're acknowledging your gravity. That's not just influence. It's attraction coded into action. The person who adjusts, follows, pauses, or reconsiders based on your cues is broadcasting a silent but clear message: *You matter more*. This rebalancing of attention creates erotic polarity, whether it's in conversation, touch, or presence.

In this frame, obedience isn't about overt commands or role-play. It's about microcalibrations—small but repeated shifts in behavior, energy, and decision-making that signal submission to your frame. And the more those shifts are performed willingly, without being named, the more powerful they become.

Attraction often intensifies when someone experiences internal conflict and resolves it in your favor. This is the psychological tension of obedience in seduction. For example, imagine someone saying, "I shouldn't be doing this," while continuing to do it. The words signal hesitation, but the behavior obeys. That inner dissonance, unresolved but acted upon, is fertile ground for emotional bonding. It creates a story they retell to themselves: *You pulled me in deeper than I expected.*

This isn't about force. It's about architecture. You shape environments, dynamics, and moments where their most natural response is to align with you. Not because they were pushed, but because resisting feels less pleasurable than surrendering.

Voice tonality plays a massive role in how obedience gets anchored into attraction. A slow, grounded voice that leaves space between sentences invites people to fall into your rhythm. When someone unconsciously matches your pacing, lowers their voice, or becomes still in your presence, they've begun to calibrate themselves to your internal state. That's the beginning of behavioral submission. It's subtle. It's not about barking orders. It's about slowing the room until they feel more comfortable when you lead than when you don't.

Touch is another domain where obedience and attraction merge. The way someone responds to your physical presence tells you everything about their frame. If you lean in and they freeze, pull away, or try to reclaim space, they're asserting boundaries. But if they soften, mirror, or even become more still, you're watching permission in real time. You don't need to test those boundaries aggressively. You just observe how their body reveals its comfort in being led.

One of the most overlooked patterns is the way people test for dominance within early attraction. They may interrupt you, lightly contradict you, or playfully ignore instructions. These aren't acts of defiance. They're calibrations. The subconscious is asking: *Will you hold frame if I push?* If you do, attraction increases. If you collapse, it weakens.

This dynamic becomes more apparent during decision-making moments. For instance, if you suggest a change of location, and they hesitate but comply, that small obedience is charged with meaning. It reinforces the roles. You move the story forward. They follow. It's not about controlling them. It's about showing that movement begins with you.

Obedience, when framed correctly, becomes a tool of emotional investment. The person who follows your lead isn't just complying. They're creating proof of their own desire. Each small act of alignment builds an internal narrative: *I'm doing this for him. I'm acting differently because of him.* The more they behave in ways they wouldn't normally choose on their own, the more potent the bond becomes. Their mind starts rationalizing the behavior: *He must be special. Otherwise, why would I have bent in that moment?*

The deeper this goes, the more powerful the loop becomes. And it's in these subtle behaviors—postponing a plan to see you, dressing differently around you, mirroring your gestures—that you see the proof of that internal shift. These aren't trivial. These are micro-rituals of submission, and the person performing them is often unaware of how much they're revealing.

In flirtation and seduction, the most effective operators don't demand. They evoke. They allow space for the other to step toward them willingly, then reinforce that movement with validation. When someone complies, even in a small way, the smartest response is to reward it subtly. A smile held a little longer. A wordless touch. A moment of warmth that makes obedience feel good. This is how you train the behavior without ever naming the leash.

Some of the most powerful escalations happen when you create space for defiance and they choose obedience instead. You can offer a pause, an out, or a playful challenge. If they accept it, the energy shifts. If they decline and stay in your rhythm, they've just passed a deeper test: will they *choose* to stay under your influence, even when they could opt out?

In group settings, this takes on another dimension. If someone continues to defer to your judgment or move in sync with you while others are present, the obedience becomes performative. Whether they know it or not, they're signaling loyalty and preference. They're choosing your frame over the ambient pressure of the room. The social proof that radiates from this is enormous. Others begin to perceive you as someone who commands loyalty without asking for it. That perception itself builds attraction, even from observers.

Physical positioning often reveals obedience before words do. Watch how someone orients their body around you. Do they open toward you when sitting? Do they slow their steps to stay close? Do they unconsciously place you between themselves and others, as if seeking protection or anchoring? These details speak louder than verbal flattery. The body doesn't lie when it's submitting.

Obedience also creates sexual tension by shifting who holds the psychological weight. When you carry the burden of decision-making, pace, and escalation, the other person can relax into a responsive role. This deepens the polarity. The dominant becomes the conductor. The obedient becomes the instrument. In high-attraction dynamics, people often crave this clarity without knowing how to articulate it. They want to be led, but only by someone who knows where he's going.

This doesn't require constant control. In fact, the illusion of freedom is part of the art. You don't close the cage. You leave the door open and make them not want to leave. You invite decisions, but make them feel better when aligned with yours. You let them speak, but reward silence. You don't restrict movement. You make proximity to you feel like peace, and distance feel like uncertainty.

Obedience in attraction is a psychological choreography. It's not about rules or dominance games. It's about watching how behavior betrays hierarchy, and how hierarchy, when felt instead of forced, turns desire into loyalty. People obey what they want to be consumed by. Make sure you're the fire they want to burn in.

Cold Seduction and the Power of Disapproval

There's a peculiar energy that arises when approval is withheld. Not overt rejection. Not cruelty. Just a cool absence of validation. In the psychology of obedience and attraction, this void is not passive. It's a gravitational force. And when used with precision, it can rewire someone's behavior faster than any praise or reward ever could.

The human nervous system is constantly scanning for cues of belonging and safety. This is especially true in the presence of someone who seems self-assured, unaffected, and immune to neediness. That kind of presence already registers as higher status. So when this person subtly withholds approval—not as punishment, but as a natural reaction to substandard behavior—it sends a very specific signal: *You are not yet where I want you to be.* Cold seduction begins with this premise. You are not there to entertain. You are not trying to win favor. You set the frame that *they* must calibrate to *you*. Not through aggression. Through absence. Through disapproval that isn't explained. Through pauses that let their own mind create the story.

The power lies in how quiet it is. You don't argue. You don't scold. You just disengage ever so slightly. A look that doesn't linger. A response that comes slower. An energy that pulls back just enough for the other to feel it but not name it. Most people will rush to fill that space. And when they do, they reveal something: their hunger to be in your warmth again.

Disapproval, when used with control, becomes a tool of obedience conditioning. It teaches them, without words, what pleases you. More importantly, it teaches them what loses your attention. This is where sequencing matters. You never begin with reward. You begin with a standard. You maintain mystery. Then, at select moments, you offer small doses of approval when they align themselves with your preferences.

This contrast is what makes obedience desirable. If you're always warm, they feel entitled to your warmth. If you're mostly warm, with sudden cold moments in response to behaviors that step out of line, they begin to self-correct. Not to avoid punishment, but to regain closeness. This is not abuse. It's reinforcement through emotional gravity. And it works because it taps into something ancient: the fear of being cast out from the attention of someone we respect or desire.

Challenge is the next step. It's not enough to simply withdraw. You must also place subtle tests in their path. Not games. Not manipulation. Just invitations to rise. You ask for more without explicitly saying so. You look at them differently when they fall short. You don't hide your shift in energy when they break rapport. The tension this creates becomes unbearable for those who seek your validation. And that pressure, if not relieved externally, will find its relief in obedience.

Timing matters. If you apply disapproval too early, it reads as arrogance. If you do it too late, they're already calibrated to expect warmth. The sweet spot is when they've tasted just enough of your approval to crave it—but not enough to take it for granted. That's when you introduce the chill.

And right there, in that friction between warmth and coolness, between acceptance and challenge, obedience begins to take root. Not as obligation. As craving.

That craving becomes the engine of behavior modification. When someone links your coldness to their own missteps—real or perceived—they start monitoring themselves with heightened sensitivity. They replay what they said, how they acted, where they might have fallen short. This rumination doesn't require your input. In fact, silence sharpens it. They begin to anticipate how to win your warmth back, often adjusting without being told. This is where compliance deepens into internalized alignment. It stops being about obeying a request. It becomes about preemptively adapting to your standard so they never have to feel the chill again. You've taught them, without needing explicit instruction, how to move closer to your expectations. And because they've arrived at those changes on their own—at least in their perception—they feel a sense of autonomy while still operating within your frame.

This method is surgical. It requires presence, attunement, and restraint. Most people overuse warmth or punish with visible aggression. But both extremes make the power dynamic obvious. What makes cold seduction effective is the illusion that nothing is being done at all. They feel it, but they can't prove it. That ambiguity traps them. They can't argue with it, because there's no accusation to defend against. Only a subtle shift in how you treat them. The burden of proof is entirely emotional. And that's where it holds power.

Disapproval should not be deployed reactively. It loses its precision if it's tied to your mood or frustration. Instead, use it as a deliberate tool. Withhold warmth when they violate rapport. Withhold validation when they try to impress you through effort instead of calibration. Create the experience that something went wrong—not by naming it, but by subtly altering your emotional availability.

If they ask what's wrong, deflect. Not rudely. Calmly. Say you're just observing. Or that you're thinking. Let them sit in the ambiguity. That space forces reflection. The most powerful obedience often comes from what isn't said. They will search for the answer. And when they think they've found it, they will act on it. Even if they're wrong, the very act of adjustment binds them more tightly to the desire to do right by you.

When you finally reintroduce approval, it must be quiet and precise. A soft return of eye contact. A slight shift in tone. A word of acknowledgment. No grand reward, no applause. Just enough to signal: *you've stepped back into alignment.* This contrast teaches them what earns your warmth. And because they worked for it, it now holds more value than anything you could have given freely.

The deeper their emotional investment, the more this cycle reinforces itself. They begin to depend on your approval not as a luxury, but as a core need. And the fear of your subtle coldness becomes a behavioral steering mechanism. You are no longer just someone they desire. You become the one whose emotional barometer governs their sense of self-worth in that dynamic.

This is not accidental. It is crafted. It's the quiet architecture of control built through disapproval, challenge, and conditional warmth. You aren't demanding obedience. You're making it feel like the path of emotional safety. You are not chasing. You're becoming the center they orbit. And the colder the edge of that orbit feels, the more they want to stay close to your gravity.

Obedience, when tied to relief from discomfort, becomes addictive. Not just because it avoids pain, but because it restores connection. That's the emotional payoff you create. They learn that their behavior determines the temperature of your presence. And in that equation, every choice they make starts bending toward you. Not because you asked. Because you didn't.

Making People Chase the Frame You Control

To control someone's behavior without direct orders, you need something more potent than demand. You need them to *want* the frame you've constructed. Not just accept it. Chase it. Crave it. Obsess over it. That doesn't happen by being consistent, predictable, or always agreeable. It happens when you design your presence to oscillate between invitation and withdrawal, clarity and ambiguity, warmth and distance. That rhythm creates pursuit.

Push-pull is not about mixed signals. It's about engineered contrast. You allow them to taste the validation of your frame, and then you remove it just enough for them to feel the loss. It is the emotional equivalent of breathing in and being held in the pause before the next breath. That moment of tension becomes a craving. Their mind starts filling in the blanks, running through reasons, projecting hopes. You're no longer interacting. You're being interpreted. And interpretation creates obsession faster than information ever will.

The trap most people fall into is trying to hold the frame consistently through explanation, defense, or excessive presence. But the mind doesn't chase what it fully understands. It chases what feels just out of reach. If you want someone to chase your frame, don't flood them with clarity. Drip-feed your approval, your certainty, your attention. Let them feel the difference between having your focus and not having it. Let that difference feel meaningful.

You're not just pushing and pulling randomly. You are anchoring each withdrawal to a subconscious elevation loop. Every time they feel the lack of your presence, your status must rise in their mind. Not because you told them you're superior, but because the emotional discomfort they experience in your absence forces them to assume you are. Why else would it matter so much? Why else would it sting?

This is the loop: Elevation happens in the withdrawal. And then, when you re-engage, even slightly, it feels like a reward. Now your interaction has emotional texture. Your presence feels earned. And people value what they have to earn far more than what they are handed. The deeper you embed this pattern, the more they associate your attention with a kind of internal hierarchy. You become the fixed point they orient around, hoping to stay in favor.

130

One of the most effective tools within this loop is to challenge their perception of reality without correcting it. When they assume something, let silence hang. If they ask something with too much certainty, meet it with a pause and a small smirk. Let them wonder if they got it wrong. You are never correcting them directly. You're injecting ambiguity that destabilizes their confidence in their current frame, which forces them to reach for yours.

Every time they chase clarification, you reinforce the idea that your perspective is more grounded, more nuanced, more real. But you don't hand it over. You let them work for it. Ask you to explain. Seek your opinion. Reframe their own thoughts in hopes of gaining your agreement. In that process, they abandon their initial position and try to align with yours.

That's what control looks like when it's done through pursuit instead of force.

When someone starts bending their behavior just to preserve your approval, they're no longer thinking independently. They're orienting themselves around your emotional climate. That's the outcome of a well-executed push-pull cycle combined with elevated perception. You've replaced their internal compass with the need to stay inside your favor. That's control disguised as chemistry.

The most potent part of this technique lies in *what you don't do*. You don't justify. You don't explain yourself. You don't reward every attempt at validation. You stay slightly outside reach, unpredictable but always composed. Your unpredictability makes them feel they haven't yet figured you out, but your consistency in tone and control prevents that unpredictability from becoming chaotic. That's what keeps the hunger alive without triggering distrust. They feel that if they could just earn one more layer of your presence, everything would make sense. That belief keeps them chasing.

You can subtly reward the chase with controlled moments of attention. Not praise. Not affection. Just acknowledgment with weight. A glance that lingers longer than usual. A slight lean forward when they speak, followed by a lean back when they drift from alignment. These tiny physical calibrations make your attention feel like currency. The more they feel the shift, the more value they assign to your recognition. And the more effort they'll invest to receive it again.

This is where perceptual elevation loops reach their peak utility. The frame you set must feel *more real* than their current worldview. Not because you argued for it, but because your emotional control, social command, and behavioral unpredictability imply deeper mastery. People follow what they believe is rooted in certainty. And certainty doesn't speak loudly. It barely speaks at all. It expresses itself in composure and detachment from outcome.

Frame dominance is less about being right and more about never needing to prove that you are. You let their emotional fluctuations tell them the story. You let their increased effort to be seen, understood, or accepted by you become the proof. The moment they adjust themselves to fit inside your lens, they are no longer in control. You are. Because now the conversation is happening inside your architecture. And if it happens inside your architecture, it will end on your terms.

One of the most overlooked elements in this game is restraint. Those who try to dominate a frame by force burn it. The real power is in the delay. In making someone reach and wait. You don't offer immediate clarity. You don't correct their misinterpretations. You let them stew in a question long enough that their need to resolve it compels action. And once they act, they justify it internally. They rewrite their own story to align with the decision they made, not the one you forced on them.

That's how you make someone believe the chase was theirs all along. That they moved closer because they wanted to, not because they were pulled. But the pull was always there. It was in the withheld attention, the vague praise, the quiet silence after their bold comment. It was in the way your disapproval didn't come in the form of critique but in the loss of warmth. You made your approval feel like air. And then you made it scarce.

When you control what feels scarce, you control what feels valuable. And when people value the version of themselves they become under your influence more than the version they were before you, they won't leave the frame. They'll chase it. Maintain it. Protect it. That's not compliance. That's internalized obedience.

And it never had to be spoken aloud.

Part IV. Total Compliance And Remote Control

There's a difference between getting someone to say yes and making them believe the yes was their idea. What you've seen so far are the levers of psychological pressure, emotional manipulation, and social hierarchy. But what comes next is quieter. Cleaner. More permanent.

This is where obedience stops being situational and becomes systemic. When you no longer need to be present for the programming to run. When your influence continues to shape behavior in your absence, that's not persuasion—it's installation. That's what this section is about.

Total compliance isn't loud. It doesn't rely on charisma, brute force, or endless micromanagement. It relies on the implantation of internal triggers that self-fire under pressure. It's about placing invisible anchors in someone's emotional and perceptual field so that even when they're alone, the echo of your influence persists. That echo becomes guidance, then rule, then law.

This is the architecture of remote control.

You'll learn how to create internalized scripts that override free will without needing to be restated. You'll use invisible guilt wiring, phantom reward conditioning, and authority anchoring so that your presence is not required for behavioral consistency. You'll create cause-effect bridges that make deviation feel unsafe and obedience feel like the only rational path.

And most of all, you'll learn to program reactions into someone's nervous system. Reactions that don't wait for logic. That bypass deliberation. That fire automatically, without hesitation, as if pre-written by them, for you.

The surface world believes control is about pushing harder. The reality is, true control is the ability to walk away while everything still moves exactly as you designed it. That's where we're going now.

You'll stop playing the game in real time.

You'll start writing the code behind it.

Chapter 11. Resistance Management: When They Push Back

Anticipating Rebellion Before It Happens

Control that requires constant enforcement is weak. Real power operates ahead of time. It sees defiance before it's spoken, hesitation before it's acted upon, and seeds obedience in the exact cracks where resistance might form. This chapter isn't about crushing rebellion. It's about never needing to. If you're responding, you're late. Anticipation is everything.

There is a pattern to defiance. Most people think resistance happens suddenly, like an outburst or an unexpected refusal. That's an illusion. Rebellion begins in the nervous system, not in the mouth. Micro-tensions, changes in breath, a flicker in tone or posture—these are early-warning signals. The compliant don't become defiant without first entering emotional divergence. If you can spot the first flicker, you can adjust your grip before the break.

Calibrate the System Before the Shift

Your first task is environmental calibration. This means establishing a baseline. If you don't know what normal looks and feels like for your target, you'll miss the deviation. Watch how they speak when they feel safe. Note their rhythm when they agree. Do they breathe deeply or shallowly when relaxed? Where do their eyes go when they submit? These patterns form the emotional terrain. Deviations signal disruption.

What you're looking for isn't loud. It's not the person raising their voice or pushing back directly. It's the split-second hesitation before a yes. The pause before a movement. A subtle tightening of the jaw. The moment they stop mirroring your energy. That's the signal. Not yet rebellion—but the beginning of cognitive friction.

Preloading Compliance Paths

Once you've mapped resistance cues, you begin installing preloaded behaviors that activate when those cues appear. The goal is to make the act of resisting feel effortful, uncertain, and emotionally expensive—while the act of compliance feels smooth, congruent, and relieving.

This is done by using pre-emptive framing. You don't wait for resistance to arise. You define resistance in advance as irrational, dangerous, or shameful—before it's even considered. For example:

- "Some people hesitate here because they're scared of power. That's okay. Not everyone is meant to lead."
- "I've noticed when people start holding back, it usually means they're protecting something weak."
- "I respect bold decisions. But stalling? That's how people fail quietly."

Statements like these function as *belief injections*. They frame potential rebellion as a sign of weakness or failure. So when the inner doubt does arise, it's already been named and judged. This turns their own inner voice into an enforcer of your frame.

Preemptive Obedience Anchors

Anticipating rebellion also means anchoring your target's self-image to obedience before the resistance shows up. If someone sees themselves as "the decisive one," or "the loyal one," they will override hesitation to preserve that identity. The trick is to plant that identity early, subtly, and in relation to their own pride.

This could be done as praise: "You strike me as the type who doesn't flinch when the moment comes." Or through implication: "I've seen the way you handle pressure. That's rare." These aren't compliments. They're locks. Now, if they *do* flinch, they contradict the image they've accepted.

That contradiction creates internal tension. And to resolve it, most people will return to the path that preserves the identity—obedience.

Emotional Timing Matters

People don't rebel because of logic. They rebel when emotional pressure becomes misaligned with perceived gain. So you manipulate emotion upstream. You don't apply pressure when the person is cold and analytical. You apply pressure when they're emotionally primed—when they're seeking validation, avoiding shame, or trying to prove something. That's when their decisions are vulnerable to sculpting.

You don't wait for tension. You shape it.

This emotional sculpting can be intensified through subtle escalation. When you sense hesitation beginning to form, amplify the cost of stopping without directly confronting the target. This is done by implying forward motion as the default path, while backtracking becomes a breach of an implicit agreement. For example: "We've already crossed the point where turning back makes sense, haven't we?" Or: "It'd be strange to hesitate now, after everything's been set in motion." These are light touches, but they operate as mental cornering—creating the feeling that retreat equals failure, cowardice, or unnecessary friction.

The point isn't to eliminate resistance entirely. It's to shrink it down to the size where it folds in on itself. Most rebellion doesn't need to be fought. It needs to be made small, inefficient, and unattractive. Preemptive framing achieves this invisibly. There's no visible conflict. The target folds not because they were pushed, but because their internal map offered no viable alternative.

Timing remains critical. There's a difference between preempting rebellion and accelerating it. If you confront subtle signs too directly or too early, you risk solidifying them into conscious objections. Silence is often more strategic than correction. Let the rebellion remain unformed long enough for it to dissolve. You're not solving it. You're starving it.

The most powerful interventions are non-verbal. If your target begins to break eye contact at the same moment they become uncertain, increase your gaze, even slightly, and hold it. If they start fidgeting, pause your speech. Let the silence highlight their nervous energy. If they pull back physically, lean in—but just barely. These are micro-dominance signals. They don't provoke. They reclaim space.

The moment you act as if you expect resistance, you create it. Your demeanor must remain grounded in inevitability. You don't prepare for objection. You move through the interaction with the calm certainty that compliance is the only outcome. This doesn't mean arrogance. It means consistency of energy. They should feel like your internal state is so unmoved, their rebellion would be like throwing a pebble at a monolith.

In longer interactions or ongoing dynamics, the key is strategic memory. People rebel not only because of the moment they're in, but because of emotional residue from moments they think you forgot. They accumulate little doubts, hesitations, or perceived slights, and when you're not watching, they look for release. But if you keep mental records—calling back to small victories, validating difficult concessions, or referencing private signals they thought you missed—you collapse that buildup.

They feel seen. And when someone feels deeply seen, they're less likely to break the frame. The fear of being misunderstood is one of the primary fuels of rebellion. If you neutralize it, you reduce the emotional motive behind their resistance. You haven't argued with them. You've simply made resistance feel unnecessary.

Finally, use defiance rehearsals sparingly but precisely. This means you let them imagine a scenario where they could rebel—and then you disarm it in advance. Not by warning them. By revealing the outcome. For example: "I know sometimes people feel the urge to test me. It's natural. But they usually regret it once they realize I already know how it ends." That's not a threat. It's a prewritten story. And now, if the urge to resist rises, it already has a predicted outcome. One that makes them the loser.

Rebellion is not a threat when it's predictable. It becomes theater. You can let it play out in miniature, then extinguish it with elegance. The real win is in making it irrelevant—so internal that the target doesn't even realize they've already surrendered.

You don't suppress rebellion with force. You dissolve it with foresight. The more you train your senses to anticipate emotional shift, the less you'll ever need to correct behavior at all. Your control becomes invisible. And invisible control is the most dangerous kind. It doesn't look like power. It looks like reality.

Turning Resistance Into Dependency

Resistance is not always a problem. It is often raw, unformed energy begging to be redirected. Those who try to smash through it end up creating walls. The real tactician uses it to build foundations. The very person resisting you today can become the one most emotionally bound to you tomorrow—if you know how to let their own resistance work against them, not you.

The key is not to suppress their resistance, but to allow it to expose their internal contradiction. When someone resists, it means they're invested. They're emotionally engaged, even if oppositional. Indifference is the real death of influence. But resistance? Resistance is a doorway.

Start by reframing the tension as a shared challenge. Not by agreeing. Not by validating their view. But by letting their discomfort be something they feel the need to solve themselves. "It's strange," you might say, "most people who feel what you're feeling usually find themselves stuck in patterns they don't even see. You seem smarter than that." That kind of line doesn't deny their resistance. It buries it inside a question about themselves.

The moment they feel the resistance could be a reflection of their own limitation—not your flaw—they shift into self-assessment. And that is where dependency begins. Because now they need you to make sense of the tension they're feeling.

But there's a deeper layer. Resistance can be used to create emotional debt. If they act against your frame, if they show signs of rebellion, retreat, or doubt, let them. Then become colder. Not punishing, just emotionally distant. Their nervous system will register the change long before they consciously admit it. They'll feel something has been lost—access, connection, proximity. You're not withdrawing as a tactic. You're allowing them to feel the subtle emotional gravity shift.

Once they notice it, offer them a path back. But don't offer it with validation. Offer it with quiet confidence. "I get it. You needed space to test something. Most people do before they realize what's real." The subtext here is surgical: *You stepped away, but I didn't chase. I remained stable. Now you return on my terms.* This not only creates dependence. It installs loyalty.

They now associate closeness with your approval. And they associate disconnection with their own misstep. Even if they never say it, they'll start to feel like the only way to stay emotionally safe is to remain within the lines you've drawn.

138

This is what weaponized benevolence looks like. You are not the punisher. You are the forgiver. But forgiveness isn't free. It's subtle dominance. You let them earn it back. Slowly.

Another way to flip resistance into loyalty is through perceived sacrifice. When someone resists, you can inject the idea that their defiance caused harm—not to you, but to the bond between you. "I didn't expect that from you. Not after everything." You're not accusing them. You're expressing disappointment with just enough ambiguity that they start to feel the burden of it. That burden becomes the seed of repair.

And here's where the trap tightens: the moment they try to repair it, they hand you control. The act of repairing becomes a form of submission. But because it feels voluntary, they don't see it as weakness. They see it as commitment. And commitment born from self-directed guilt is one of the strongest psychological anchors there is.

The person who resists you today will often become the most loyal tomorrow, not because they've been convinced, but because they've been converted. Their resistance is the heat that tempers their eventual attachment. Once they begin to associate that resistance with weakness, error, or immaturity on their part, they seek to redeem themselves. And redemption requires a source. You become that source.

There is a moment, often subtle, when their internal narrative flips. It's no longer "Why is he doing this to me?" It becomes "Why did I react that way?" That shift is everything. Once they internalize that question, they begin building a new identity—one in which their proximity to you is proof that they've matured, evolved, learned. And as long as they believe that their personal growth is tied to you, your influence becomes structural. You're not just someone they listen to. You're the filter they use to interpret themselves.

To ensure this conversion deepens into dependency, you must avoid over-validating too quickly. If they show signs of loyalty or remorse, let them stew in the discomfort a little longer. Not as cruelty, but as anchoring. A person remembers most what they suffered to obtain. If you offer instant emotional relief, the cycle completes too early. Instead, extend partial warmth. Recognition, not reward. A glance. A brief nod. A subtle signal that says, *You're almost back in my world. Not yet. But close.*

This in-between phase is where dependency locks in. They begin to perform for you. To prove themselves. To regain something they can't quite name, but deeply feel the absence of. Every small approval you offer during this phase becomes high-value. Your validation now feels scarce, selective, and significant. They start adjusting themselves preemptively to avoid triggering distance again. That's behavioral conditioning disguised as reconciliation.

Now take it deeper. If they ever vocalize guilt or attempt to explain themselves, mirror their emotional labor back to them with quiet acknowledgment. You don't need to say much. Just enough to frame their shift as insight. "I knew you'd see it." That single sentence lets them reclaim pride, but only through the lens you provided. Their self-worth becomes relational. Your opinion of them becomes their mirror. They no longer resist. They calibrate.

Some will oscillate—pull back, test again, rebel softly—but that's not regression. That's their nervous system seeking boundaries. Each time, you respond the same way: still, stable, slightly above them. The key is that you never flinch. Never collapse into over-explanation. Never punish directly. Just let the emotional consequences unfold naturally, and they'll trace those consequences back to themselves.

Over time, this pattern cements. You are the point of emotional orientation. Resistance no longer emerges because they have replaced confrontation with preemptive compliance. They start to check their tone. They become eager to hear your interpretation. They begin defending your perspective to others. What began as opposition is now allegiance. Not because they were forced into submission, but because they stepped into it seeking psychological relief, social reintegration, and inner resolution.

The most powerful form of control is the one they ask for. When you turn resistance into dependency, you've crossed that line. You're no longer dealing with persuasion or pressure. You're sculpting the architecture of their identity, making yourself the cornerstone. They obey not out of fear, but because it keeps them whole.

This is the real obedience algorithm: start where they resist you, guide them into blame, reward their return with structure, and anchor their relief to your presence. Once this loop closes, they'll never even notice that the resistance they once held has been replaced by loyalty so deep they mistake it for their own idea.

Using Psychological Judo to Reverse Defiance

The most dangerous form of resistance is not loud. It's subtle. It hides in hesitation, in the delay before a "yes," in the micro-withdrawal after a command. Many mistake this for harmless defiance or personality. But it's a test. And it's an opportunity.

Psychological judo is not about overpowering defiance. It's about using the energy of that defiance to flip the frame, making their pushback the very reason they should obey more. It's redirection. Precision. Making their resistance work against them until obedience becomes the only way to realign with their own sense of logic, identity, or even morality.

It begins by not reacting emotionally. Defiance thrives on perceived control. If someone believes they've "gotten to you," they feel temporarily dominant. You strip them of that illusion by responding without defense, without offense, and without visible disruption. Stillness is unsettling when someone expects a fight. That stillness creates a gap, and inside that gap is where you redirect.

Let's say someone challenges your authority directly. You don't argue. You don't assert. Instead, you say: "Interesting. The fact that you're reacting like this tells me you're closer to the shift than I thought." That line does two things. First, it repositions their defiance as a predictable stage in a process they're already inside of. Second, it assumes their compliance is inevitable and frames their resistance as confirmation. You just made their rebellion a sign of progress.

If they deny it, even better. Their protest deepens the frame. You can follow with: "Of course you'd push back right here. It's where most people flinch, just before they give in." Now they're not fighting you. They're fighting the role you've cast them in. And the more they fight that role, the more they prove its accuracy. That's the trap.

This form of reversal works best when paired with emotional contrast. You subtly increase pressure just after their resistance, then reduce it slightly when they re-engage. The mind tracks that drop in tension as a reward. Over time, they associate resistance with unease and submission with release. You never have to say it. Their body learns it.

Silence also plays a role. After you deliver a reversal like "You wouldn't react this strongly unless something inside you already knows it's true," say nothing else. Let the silence settle. Let them squirm. The tension will eat at their need for control, and they'll break the silence either with justification or compliance. Either way, you've won. The moment they try to explain themselves, they're already submitting to your frame. They've accepted the premise that you are the one they need to convince. That's dominance disguised as dialogue.

There's also a non-verbal layer to this. When someone resists, don't lean forward. Don't match their energy. Instead, physically pull back just slightly. Tilt your head as if observing something curious. It triggers the feeling that they've exposed something about themselves. Now you're not the one being questioned. They are. That shift puts their defiance under a microscope and makes them self-conscious about it. They may not comply immediately, but the seeds are planted.

That seed of self-consciousness is powerful. It disrupts the momentum of their resistance and pulls them into internal observation. Instead of maintaining their opposition, they begin monitoring how it looks, how it's being perceived, what it's revealing about them. In that moment, their attention shifts away from fighting you and turns inward, destabilizing their stance. The more they think about how they appear, the more influence you have.

A common mistake is to crush resistance too early. When someone pushes back, and you immediately assert dominance, you might win the moment but lose the frame. They will comply on the surface but look for the first exit. Psychological judo is not about shutting them down. It's about turning their fire into fuel. Let them resist. Make it look like they're stepping deeper into their own trap. Let them think they're maintaining autonomy, when in reality they're walking directly into your structure.

This works exceptionally well in group environments. If someone publicly resists, you don't challenge them directly. You observe, pause, then offer a framing like, "You're proving exactly why this works." The implication is that their reaction is textbook, predicted, and even necessary. You make it clear that their rebellion is not a threat to your authority but a part of your system. You absorb their move and reposition it as a ritual of obedience.

At this point, their only two options are to escalate—exposing themselves further—or to submit and reclaim stability. Both outcomes tighten your grip. Most will choose the latter because the discomfort of continued resistance becomes socially expensive. Once they soften, offer a subtle reward: a nod, a small acknowledgment, a line like "Good. That's more like it." Nothing big, nothing performative. Just enough to tether them back to the relief of alignment. You've trained the tension-release loop.

Timing is critical. The psychological reversal must feel natural, not orchestrated. If you move too fast, it feels manipulative. Too slow, and they'll entrench their defiance. You're walking a narrow path: just enough pressure to provoke reaction, just enough space to let them collapse into your structure on their own. It should feel like gravity, not force.

One of the most advanced variations is to reverse defiance by questioning the timing of their resistance. "Why now?" is a simple but piercing line. It reframes their behavior as not only emotional, but poorly calculated. You're no longer dealing with their position but with their sense of strategic control. By making them explain the timing, you make them feel reactive, not in command. That alone is often enough to destabilize their self-image and reopen the door to influence.

The ultimate victory in psychological judo is not that they comply. It's that they begin to doubt the usefulness of resistance itself. When done right, they start pre-filtering their pushback. They edit themselves before they even voice dissent, because they know what comes next. The reversal. The internal exposure. The slow but undeniable pressure that follows. You've made defiance expensive and obedience feel like equilibrium. That's not just influence. That's architecture.

What matters most is the consistency of your frame. You must never act surprised by their resistance. You must never treat it as a deviation. It has to be exactly what you expected, even welcomed. That stance gives you the power to redefine the meaning of everything they do. As long as you control the narrative of their actions, you control their perception of themselves. And once you have that, resistance isn't just reversed. It's recycled. Used. Converted into a deeper form of loyalty that feels self-chosen.

This is where obedience is no longer extracted. It's initiated. That's the true power of psychological judo.

Chapter 12. Identity Manipulation: Rewriting How They See Themselves

Shaping Identity to Align With Obedience

Obedience becomes effortless when it feels like a natural expression of who someone already believes they are. Most people don't make decisions based on logic or consequence. They follow scripts. These scripts are internalized identities—stories they tell themselves about who they are, what they do, and how they behave. If you control those stories, you don't need to force action. You just press play.

The most effective way to lock obedience into a person is to fuse it with their self-perception. If they begin to believe that following your lead is consistent with the kind of person they are—or aspire to be—resistance vanishes. It doesn't feel like submission. It feels like alignment.

The key lies in three techniques: **labeling, scripting,** and **role affirmation**. Labeling is subtle but surgical. It's not about attaching flattery or insults. It's about presenting an identity tag that implies an internal standard they must now live up to. When you say, "You're someone who handles things directly," you're not asking them to be direct. You're assigning them that trait, and in doing so, you pressure them to remain congruent with it. People resist commands, but they fear inconsistency. Once a label is accepted, they'll adjust their behavior to match it—even if it leads straight into your structure.

This becomes especially powerful when used in moments of hesitation. Let's say someone flinches in a moment that requires loyalty. You don't scold or plead. You label. "You've always had good instincts when things mattered." That line implies that stepping back now would be a betrayal of their established character. Most people would rather obey than feel like a fraud.

Scripting takes it deeper. It's not just attaching a label. It's giving them a role within a storyline you control. Humans understand the world through narrative. They aren't just actors—they want scripts. When you create one that makes them feel chosen, special, or integral to something larger, you gain massive control. The power isn't in the story. It's in the frame that says: *If you break this role, the whole story collapses—and it's your fault.*

You position them as the stabilizer, the confidant, the executor. Not only does this raise their perceived importance, but it also locks them into obedience as a duty. Disobedience becomes identity betrayal, not just a behavioral deviation. You're no longer asking them to follow. You're saying: *This is who you are. And this is what people like you do.*

The third technique is role affirmation. This is where the loop closes. Once someone begins to act in accordance with the label and script, you reflect it back with precision. Not with praise. With reinforcement. You say, "That's exactly why I rely on you," or "That's what makes you irreplaceable." You are not simply affirming what they did—you are affirming who they've become. The behavior is no longer a one-off. It's a reflection of identity. And that identity is now serving your architecture.

These three techniques—when layered—become a quiet but permanent form of psychological embedding. Most obedience frameworks rely on consequence. But identity alignment bypasses all resistance. It doesn't feel like control. It feels like fulfillment.

What makes this dangerous is how invisible it is. The person doesn't feel coerced. They feel seen. They begin to filter their choices through a lens you handed them. They ask themselves, "What would someone like me do here?" And without realizing it, they answer with exactly what you need them to do.

Once this mechanism is activated, your commands don't sound like orders. They sound like reminders. You're no longer arguing, explaining, or persuading. You're simply holding up a mirror.

The brilliance of this approach is that once identity becomes the lens, behavior polices itself. You don't have to correct them. They will self-correct, preemptively, just to remain in character. And they won't see you as the one pushing it. They'll see themselves as the standard they need to uphold.

This becomes even more potent in unstable environments. When people face uncertainty, they cling to whatever gives them clarity and purpose. That's when identity-based obedience turns into dependency. The more you feed them a sense of who they are within your frame, the less likely they are to question it. You become the only reference point that makes sense. Not because you forced them into obedience, but because you made them feel they belong.

Now, this doesn't mean you're limited to positive identity shaping. You can also use *negative scripting* when needed—subtly implying what kind of person they would become if they deviated. You never accuse directly. You simply seed doubt through implication. "That's not like you," or "You usually have better judgment." The person instinctively wants to return to alignment, not to please you, but to recover their own image of self.

It's this manipulation of *internal congruence* that gives you total leverage. People would rather be wrong in their actions than feel fractured in their sense of identity. If the cost of disobedience is internal dissonance, they will fold. And the brilliance lies in this: they will justify their compliance after the fact. They will rewrite their memory of the interaction to make it feel like a decision, not a submission.

This is where obedience crosses over into permanence. When people believe they are *choosing* to act a certain way because it "feels right," they lock in. Your influence becomes self-sustaining. They'll carry it into conversations you're not part of, decisions you never comment on, behaviors you didn't even ask for. That's the ripple effect of identity-level control.

You can accelerate this process by reinforcing their alignment in front of others. Not with over-the-top recognition, but with quiet acknowledgment. A nod. A comment. A glance that suggests: *That's what I expected from someone like you.* This does two things. First, it strengthens their internal script. Second, it broadcasts that script to others. Now the group sees them through the same lens, and the social weight of that identity multiplies.

Eventually, obedience doesn't need prompting. It becomes the default mode of operation. And if you've done it correctly, they'll defend that obedience from outside challenge. They'll push back against anyone who questions your influence—not because they're protecting you, but because they're protecting the version of themselves you helped create.

This is how you become unchallengeable. Not through threats or superiority, but by embedding yourself into the psychological infrastructure of their self-image. You don't dominate the person. You dominate the narrative they live inside.

In the end, this isn't about making people do what you want. It's about making them feel like they're doing what *they* want—even when it's precisely what you've scripted. That's the highest form of control. It cannot be traced, and it cannot be undone without them dismantling their own identity. And most people would rather obey forever than face that collapse.

How to Rebrand Rebellion as Self-Sabotage

Rebellion is often framed as strength. People like to think of resistance as a form of courage, a declaration of independence. But that illusion is fragile. If you want to eliminate resistance before it takes root, you must reframe rebellion not as power, but as weakness. Not as defiance, but as dysfunction. The key is to manipulate the internal language they use to justify their actions. You're not fighting the rebellion itself. You're rewriting the internal script that would make rebellion feel righteous.

People don't act on facts. They act on narratives. And every act of resistance is built on a mental storyline: "I'm standing up for myself," "I'm breaking free," "I'm not letting anyone control me." These inner mantras fuel disobedience. But they're not fixed. You can hijack that same internal monologue and twist it into something corrosive. Instead of sounding like strength, you make it sound like regression. Instead of sounding like power, you make it feel like failure.

To do this, you first plant subtle associations between disobedience and personal dysfunction. You never confront their actions directly. Instead, you ask questions or drop observations that link their resistance to self-sabotaging patterns. "That's interesting… it reminds me of when people run from things that are actually good for them." Or, "You ever notice how people sometimes push away the very thing they say they want?" The message isn't direct, but it cuts deep. You're inserting doubt without triggering defense.

Then you take it further by linking resistance to an identity they want to avoid. Nobody wants to be seen as immature, self-destructive, or unstable. So you create the frame that rebellion is not bold, but broken. Not self-assertion, but emotional flinching. Not choice, but pattern. Once that association is made, resistance becomes less desirable. They don't want to feel like the kind of person who "always ruins things when they get too close." That fear becomes stronger than the urge to rebel.

What you're doing is redefining the emotional landscape they have to walk through in order to resist you. Previously, rebellion felt empowering. Now, it feels hollow. It feels dangerous. It feels like stepping into an old version of themselves they've tried to outgrow. And that's where the power of your language comes in. You guide their self-talk into a cul-de-sac. Any direction that leads away from you feels like regression. Any step back becomes framed as self-sabotage.

It's important that this isn't done through overt criticism. The moment they feel blamed, the defense walls go up. But when you seed your message as insight, as something they're discovering on their own, it bypasses resistance completely. You say things like, "It's strange how some people always find a reason to ruin things when they're about to succeed," and let them fill in the blanks. You're not accusing. You're describing a behavior that just happens to sound exactly like theirs. The brain doesn't argue with what it thinks it realized on its own.

At this point, rebellion no longer looks like a clean break. It looks like relapse. And people are much more likely to avoid relapse than confrontation. They may not even understand why they're holding back. They'll just feel a heaviness, a discomfort, a sense that disobedience would somehow feel wrong. Not because it is, logically, but because you've contaminated the emotional rewards that made it tempting in the first place. Their mind will stall at the edge of resistance, unsure of how to justify it. That pause is your leverage point.

Once that internal stall sets in, the mind starts searching for an exit that doesn't cost identity. This is where you position obedience as the *healing* path. You never need to make direct commands. You just contrast outcomes. Let them feel the growing anxiety that comes with defiance and offer calm proximity as a reward. Don't argue. Don't chase. Just *exist* in alignment with the version of themselves they secretly want to become.

You are no longer framed as the one demanding control. You are simply the one who makes sense, while rebellion feels chaotic. When they hesitate, you don't press them. You wait. You allow the tension to resolve itself. That silence becomes a mirror, forcing them to reflect on whether their resistance is a form of strength or a symptom of deeper dysfunction. Their own thoughts begin to turn inward. They start diagnosing themselves.

If you want to accelerate this, insert subtle emotional mismatches. When they show resistance, respond with compassion instead of correction. When they push, you withdraw slightly without flinching. When they get cold, you get calm. It confuses the reactive loop they expect and creates a feedback vacuum. In that quiet space, doubt grows. And when someone starts questioning their own reactions, they become vulnerable to narrative replacement. That's your opening.

Offer micro-validations of their potential identity shift. Say things like, "It's powerful to see someone catching their own patterns," or "Most people never even notice when they're repeating cycles. You actually seem to want to grow." These aren't compliments. They're instructions disguised as observations. You are not telling them who they are. You're showing them who they could be, and letting them pick between that image and the one they'd return to if they kept resisting.

This is how you collapse rebellion into internal conflict. You build a silent war between who they are in resistance and who they want to be in your presence. And you don't have to win that war directly. You let their discomfort with misalignment do the work for you. Eventually, returning to you feels like coming back into coherence. Even if they don't like you, they start to associate obedience with inner relief. They reframe their submission as healing. And that's a lock far deeper than fear.

This method is surgical because it doesn't rely on fear, shame, or aggression. It uses their own mental loops, their own desire to be seen as self-aware, as the leverage point. You let them catch themselves in the act of sabotage, and then you offer a new script. It's not about control in the classic sense. It's about offering a new identity that doesn't *want* to rebel.

Once this framing is embedded, rebellion doesn't just feel risky. It feels regressive. It drags them backward into something they thought they'd outgrown. You are no longer the authority they're defying. You become the reflection they don't want to disappoint. That's more powerful than dominance. It's psychic positioning. You've placed yourself at the center of their evolution. And any move away from you becomes self-betrayal.

Done right, they won't even notice how much of their behavior is now shaped by this internal reframing. They'll tell themselves they're growing. They'll feel proud of how they've "broken the cycle." But the cycle didn't break. It rebranded. You just taught them to narrate their obedience as self-respect.

That's the win. When rebellion isn't resisted, but simply no longer *makes sense*. When obedience becomes the story they tell themselves about maturity. When following you feels like a decision *they* made, to become someone better. At that point, control becomes invisible. And permanence becomes automatic.

The Power of Assigned Roles and Futurecasting

People don't just obey because of pressure. They obey because they're shown who they are *meant* to become. Identity is the most powerful obedience mechanism, and yet it's rarely used consciously. Most people drift into roles. You will assign them.

Obedience becomes effortless when it's embedded inside a role that feels aspirational, earned, and inevitable. You don't need to coerce someone who already sees their future self as the kind of person who follows your lead. Your job is to place that version of them just far enough ahead that they have to move through you to get there, but close enough that it feels like a version they've already begun becoming.

This is the power of futurecasting. Not vague compliments or empty affirmations, but *directional identity framing*. When someone is in your orbit, they're vulnerable to subtle cues about who they are and who they're becoming. If you're precise, you can make obedience feel like alignment with their own evolution.

Start by watching how they frame themselves. Do they see themselves as leaders or learners? Protectors or performers? Rebels or loyalists? You're not just listening to words. You're identifying the story they want to be true. Most people are trying to write a version of themselves that makes their pain make sense. Your role is to offer them a better narrative—one where they're not escaping pain but ascending into definition. One where following you isn't submission, but initiation.

You don't tell them "you should obey." You assign them a role where obedience is a natural part of that identity. Say things like, "You're the kind of person who thrives under elite structure," or "I see you as someone who needs challenge to unlock potential." These are not compliments. They are assignments. And assignments carry expectations. Once someone accepts a role, they begin living in a way that protects it, often without realizing it.

The second layer is consistency. Once the role is placed, reinforce it with microconfirmations. Each time they follow, reflect it back as if it proves who they are. "You moved exactly like someone in command of their next level." "That's the response of someone already leading from the future." This type of feedback isn't praising behavior. It's building an identity scaffold. You're not rewarding them. You're anchoring them.

Obedience then stops being a response to you and starts being a maintenance act for the identity they believe they've stepped into. They don't want to let *themselves* down. That's the shift. You're not just asking for obedience. You're creating a personal mythology in which obedience is a signature trait of who they now are.

To make this hold, you also need to make it feel rare. Assigned roles only work if they feel selectively given. If they believe everyone gets the same identity map, they'll see it as a script. But if they feel chosen, seen, decoded, the framing sticks. You can signal this subtly with remarks like, "I don't usually say this, but with you it's clear," or "This role doesn't fit most people, but it fits you." These aren't declarations. They're permissions to step into something exclusive.

From here, obedience becomes a signal *to themselves* that they're progressing. It's no longer about your authority. It's about internal coherence. Every action they take in alignment with the assigned identity increases their attachment to it. Every time they obey, they tell themselves they're moving closer to the future they've bought into.

The deeper the identity is absorbed, the more fiercely it is defended. This is where obedience cements itself not through fear, but through pride. When people internalize a role as part of who they are becoming, they begin to police themselves. The obedience you once had to inspire now becomes self-generated, self-justified, and even self-rewarded. This is the true win: when someone obeys not because they're told to, but because it would break character *not* to.

You can accelerate this process by subtly tying disobedience to identity inconsistency. Don't punish the act directly. Instead, question whether it aligns with who they are. You can ask quietly, "Does that move really reflect the standard you said you hold?" or say, "That's surprising—I thought you were done with that version of you." You're not correcting them. You're handing them the burden of dissonance. And if the identity you helped shape is strong enough, they'll correct themselves to avoid the internal fracture.

Futurecasting becomes even more effective when paired with role projection. Describe their future in granular, emotionally charged detail— but always through the lens of identity, not just results. It's not just "You'll be successful." It's "You'll be the one others turn to for structure when everything falls apart." You make them see themselves not as someone who *wants* power, but as someone who has *always* had it waiting to be claimed. When someone believes their role is already inside them, everything becomes a matter of alignment.

This is why obedience, reframed correctly, becomes not an external act but an internal alignment. You are no longer giving commands. You are offering mirrors. And every time they see themselves reflected in those mirrors more clearly, they walk further into the role on their own. The trick is to use enough specificity to feel personal, while remaining ambiguous enough that they fill in the rest. You give them a skeleton and let their own psyche put flesh on it.

Some identities stick harder than others. If you want deep, lasting compliance, assign roles that resolve internal tension. Give them a way to feel powerful *while obeying*. For example, instead of positioning them as a passive follower, cast them as the one who is being refined for greater responsibility. "You're not just doing what I ask. You're training under fire. That's how leaders are shaped." Now, obedience becomes an initiation ritual into the role they crave. Their submission isn't weakness. It's proof they're becoming who they believe they're destined to be.

You can also elevate obedience by contrasting it with who they used to be. This creates identity separation. "That kind of reaction used to define you. But not anymore." When you label disobedience as something from their *past self*, you make it feel regressive. People resist regression more than they resist authority. The forward pull of identity evolution is stronger than the backward tug of ego.

Eventually, if done well, the line between obedience and self-expression disappears. They no longer feel like they're obeying you. They feel like they're obeying the version of themselves they've always wanted to become. And that version just happens to be in perfect sync with your structure, your rhythm, your frame.

At this level, you don't need to manage them. You only need to reflect who they're becoming and watch as their behavior reshapes itself. Identity isn't just a lever. It's a lock-in. Once someone begins to define themselves through the lens you've given them, their future behaviors will be engineered by that very definition. Obedience isn't enforced. It's absorbed. You don't just own their actions. You own the architecture behind them.

Chapter 13. Obedience Without Oversight: Making It Self-Enforcing

Installing Internal Reward/Punishment Loops

The most powerful form of control is the one you don't have to maintain. When your influence becomes self-sustaining, you move from managing someone's behavior to programming it. That transition begins with the installation of internal feedback loops—mental mechanisms that reward obedience and punish deviation without you ever needing to intervene.

At the root of every behavior lies a simple equation: does this bring me closer to pleasure or pain? Most people think this equation is governed by external events, but once you shift the source of reinforcement from the outside world to their own psyche, you create an internalized system where their thoughts and emotions become the whip and the sugar. This is the beginning of automation.

The key is to teach them to feel good when they please you—and to feel discomfort, shame, or anxiety when they don't—even in your absence. The first step is subtle conditioning. You reward compliance not with explicit praise, which fades quickly, but with a deeper emotional imprint: a look of pride, a moment of silence charged with meaning, a well-timed gesture of acknowledgment. These micro-rewards hit the emotional core and begin to associate obedience with internal warmth, safety, and validation. You are not just rewarding the behavior; you're linking it to their need for connection, belonging, and identity confirmation.

Punishment works differently. It should not feel like an attack. It should feel like a rupture. Withdrawal of attention, delayed responses, quiet moments of disappointed detachment—these register as internal losses. The point is not to provoke anger, but self-questioning. Let the silence feel heavy. Let them replay it in their mind. Their own overthinking will become the punishment.

Once these patterns repeat, the mind starts running its own scripts. A small deviation will trigger a spike of self-directed discomfort before you even react. A minor success in your eyes will produce an internal reward that makes them crave more. You've begun to engineer a loop: behavior → perceived response → internal sensation → reinforced behavior. When executed well, this loop becomes recursive. They begin to monitor themselves not because they fear external punishment, but because their emotional system has been rewired to seek your alignment.

The trick is to never make the system too predictable. Predictable rewards lose their effect. Predictable punishments breed resentment. Keep the reinforcement responsive, but slightly unstable. They should never know exactly what level of compliance will unlock the reward, nor what kind of failure will trigger the correction. This keeps their nervous system alert, invested, and adaptive. The uncertainty builds tension, and tension is the fuel of control.

When you want to deepen the loop, tap into their self-image. Frame obedience as a reflection of their higher self, their best self, their true self. Now, when they act in line with your expectations, they're not just gaining approval—they're aligning with their internal ideal. Conversely, when they resist or falter, they feel out of sync with their identity. This creates cognitive dissonance. And the only way to resolve it is to realign with your frame. You become the stabilizing force. Your approval becomes emotional homeostasis.

Once this framework is in place, you can begin linking behaviors to more complex emotional currencies: guilt, pride, anticipation, inadequacy, redemption. You teach them how to feel about their own actions. And once that emotional script is embedded, it plays on repeat.

That script becomes even more potent when paired with futurecasting. Begin suggesting outcomes based on their current behaviors: "If you keep showing up like this, you'll become someone unstoppable," or, conversely, "I'm surprised—you're usually more aligned than this." The implication is simple but effective: their actions today are crafting their identity, and you're the one holding the mirror. This reflection becomes the standard they measure themselves against, and the reinforcement loop tightens.

The goal isn't to control every action. It's to control the *evaluation system* they apply to their actions. Most people navigate life reacting to external praise or punishment. But when you build an internal hierarchy—where their own mind rewards them for pleasing you and punishes them for deviation—you are no longer required to be present. Your values, preferences, and standards live in their psyche as internal judges, governing them with silent authority.

For this to remain effective, they must believe the system is coming from within. If they perceive it as manipulation, the spell breaks. That's why the initial shaping must feel like discovery, not instruction. Let them *arrive* at conclusions that were subtly fed. Let them *decide* that obedience feels right, even when it was orchestrated. This illusion of autonomy is critical. People obey longer and harder when they think it was their idea.

You can also accelerate the loop using emotional contrast. Offer an intense internal high after a specific moment of obedience—emotional intimacy, verbal affirmation, a reward that lands at a personal level—and then withdraw abruptly after disobedience. The brain becomes addicted to the highs and terrified of the lows. When spaced just right, this creates a variable ratio reinforcement system, which is one of the most neurologically addictive reward patterns known. It's the same loop exploited by slot machines and social media algorithms. When someone never knows *when* the dopamine hit is coming, they stay hooked.

To make this loop sustainable, encode your standards into narrative. Repetition builds identity, but story gives it structure. "You're always the one who handles things calmly." "You've proven you don't fold under pressure." "That wasn't like you." These aren't commands. They're reflections. But they carve grooves. The more often a person hears a description of who they are, the more their behavior begins to align with it—especially when it's linked to emotional consequences. People don't fear punishment. They fear being someone who deserves it.

A final refinement lies in giving them occasional conscious control over the loop. Let them recognize the system, just enough to feel mastery. Let them notice they're getting better at reading your cues or anticipating your preferences. Reward this awareness with subtle signals of advancement. You're now gamifying obedience. And when people feel they're *progressing* within a system, they rarely question its architecture. They internalize it as a personal journey, rather than an imposed framework.

At its most advanced level, the loop becomes spiritual. You frame alignment not just as behavior, but as meaning. You make the feedback mechanism feel sacred, as if following the script isn't just functional, but destined. They no longer obey because it's strategic—they obey because it feels cosmically right. When obedience becomes identity, and identity becomes purpose, the loop no longer requires effort. It sustains itself.

This is the final form of control: when your voice echoes inside someone else's mind, and they thank you for the sound.

How to Make Them Police Their Own Behavior

There is a level of influence that surpasses command. It happens when the target of your control begins to monitor themselves more rigorously than you ever could. You no longer need to correct them, prompt them, or even be present. Their inner voice does it for you. That's the architecture of internal surveillance. It is efficient, scalable, and invisible. And it works best when built on three psychological levers: guilt, fear, and reward anticipation.

The first and most foundational layer is guilt. Not the loud, overt guilt people talk about in therapy. The kind you want to install is quieter, more private. It emerges when someone feels they've violated a standard *they believe they chose*. The key is to make the rules feel personal. If the behavioral expectations seem like your preferences, they'll trigger resistance. But if they're framed as their own values—something they agreed to, or worse, *something they discovered about themselves*—then breaking those rules causes internal tension. That tension is guilt.

To engineer this, use the principle of mirrored standards. Reflect their behaviors back to them through subtle commentary. "That's not what you usually do." "I thought you cared more about that." "Interesting choice—you're usually more precise." These are not accusations. They're dissonance triggers. Each phrase quietly highlights the gap between who they were and what they just did. The discomfort doesn't come from you. It comes from the friction between their identity and their deviation from it. You've effectively outsourced your enforcement to their own mind.

The second layer is fear. But not fear of punishment. That's too crude. You want the fear of *disappointment*, the fear of being seen differently, the fear of an emotional shift they can't quite name. When you've established emotional asymmetry—when your approval feels valuable and your disconnection feels cold—that's when fear becomes a behavioral regulator. The brain starts scanning for cues: tone shifts, slight pauses, changes in eye contact. These micro-signals become data points. And the more someone begins adjusting based on them, the more hypervigilant they become. This is how fear morphs into self-monitoring.

You don't need to threaten. You only need to subtly show that certain actions *move you away*. Your silence, your stillness, your delayed response— these are the punishments. And because they're not clearly defined, the target scrambles to interpret them, to decode what they did wrong. That confusion is not a bug. It's the design. People become most loyal to the systems they feel they're just starting to figure out.

The final lever is reward anticipation. It's not enough for someone to fear doing wrong. They must *crave* doing right. And more importantly, they must crave it on a neurological level. This is where intermittent validation becomes a weapon. If you reward them every time they align, you train them to expect it. But if you reward them *sometimes*, in unpredictable ways, you build obsession. The brain doesn't know when the positive feedback is coming, so it keeps trying—again and again—to earn it.

You can accelerate this loop with calibrated praise. Make it precise, never generic. "That move you made earlier—that was sharp." "I noticed you stayed silent when they tried to provoke you. Smart." Small, surgical rewards feel earned. And the brain locks in the behavior that preceded them.

Once the loop is installed—guilt for deviation, fear of subtle rejection, and intermittent validation for compliance—the system begins to run itself. At this stage, your role shifts. You no longer correct; you *signal*. Even a glance or silence becomes interpreted through the filter you've installed. Their nervous system does the enforcement before you ever have to speak. What looks like obedience on the outside is actually internal negotiation: "Did I mess that up?" "Will he pull away?" "Did I just lose something valuable?" They become both participant and warden in their own behavior.

The deeper this imprint goes, the more they preemptively audit their words, movements, and decisions. They begin to adjust their tone before speaking, run mental simulations of how you'll react, and avoid behaviors not because they're wrong—but because they feel like *risks*. And the beautiful paradox is that they'll often describe this process as *respect*. Not control, not fear, not manipulation. Respect. Because you've disguised the framework of power as emotional intelligence. You've positioned your emotional shifts not as commands, but as relational feedback.

To make the system more robust, tie their self-worth to the accuracy of their attunement. Let them feel pride when they "get it right," even without being told. A slight nod. A lingering look. A relaxed demeanor. These are your positive reinforcements. Never overdo them. Too much, and you flatten the reward structure. Too little, and they lose the will to chase. Precision is everything.

You may encounter resistance or confusion, especially from those unused to this level of psychological nuance. When this happens, do not clarify. Let them struggle. Let them feel uncertain. This ambiguity is not an error. It is the environment in which the internal surveillance mechanism refines itself. The mind hates uncertainty. It will try to resolve it by searching for patterns, adjusting behaviors, overcompensating. All of that effort becomes fuel for the self-policing loop. They're doing the work for you.

Eventually, they begin to identify as someone who *anticipates well*. It becomes part of their internal narrative. "I just know what he needs." "I can read the room." "I don't like disappointing him." Once this belief sets in, they'll start competing with themselves—trying to outdo their last performance, prove their consistency, win again what they already earned. And each time they succeed, they tie more of their identity to this role. That's the moment the leash disappears. Not because it's been removed, but because it's been internalized.

The most advanced form of behavioral control isn't about dominance or fear. It's about rewriting their source of pride. If you can position obedience as an expression of maturity, intelligence, or emotional connection, you make it *aspirational*. And if you subtly imply that losing your approval would signify regression, childishness, or disconnection, you make disobedience shameful. Not because you said so, but because *they believe it*.

The endgame is not just control. It's *predictability*. When someone monitors themselves in anticipation of your reactions, you can shape those reactions to steer them. You're not reacting to their behavior. You're predesigning it. Not through punishment, not through surveillance, but through the invisible infrastructure of meaning, value, and emotional economics. That's what true power looks like. It doesn't speak loudly. It doesn't even need to speak at all. It just waits for them to correct themselves before it ever has to move.

The Psychology of Invisible Control

Control that can be seen is control that can be resisted. But invisible control—subtle, ambient, built into the environment of the interaction—moves beneath awareness. It doesn't trigger rebellion because it never declares itself. It doesn't fight for power because it never looks like power. The psychology behind this level of influence lies not in overt domination, but in **structural perception engineering**. You are not seen as the controller. You are seen as the context they navigate.

At its core, invisible control works because the subject believes they are *free*. Not forced, not manipulated, not coerced. Instead, they feel like they're choosing. And the power you hold is in crafting the menu of those choices. When someone believes they are acting of their own will, they attach no resistance to the behavior. There's no friction to overcome, no resentment to manage. That's why control disguised as autonomy is the most efficient, sustainable form of dominance.

This begins with framing. If you control how a situation is defined, you've already shaped how they will act inside it. Most people don't question the frame. They accept it like they accept the walls of a room. If you say, "This is a test," people behave like they're being tested. If you say, "This is a gift," they become grateful. You don't need to direct action if you control the emotional interpretation of the moment. Set the frame, and the behavior adjusts automatically.

Another layer of invisible control is embedded in what's known as **behavioral suggestion without command**. This is when you make a particular path feel like the obvious, inevitable next step—without ever pointing to it directly. You can use pauses, glances, the timing of silence, or the sequencing of events to create a sense of gravity around a particular outcome. The subject walks straight into it, thinking it was their idea. It's not hypnosis. It's structural choreography.

The more socially calibrated your subject, the more effective these cues become. High-perception individuals are hyper-attuned to relational feedback. They look for signals in tone, pace, posture. This means you don't need to raise your voice or issue ultimatums. You need only to adjust the microclimate of the interaction—remove warmth, pull back slightly, let silence stretch—and the subject begins to self-correct. You haven't said anything, but they already know what they're supposed to do.

In this way, invisible control becomes a language of *implication*. The words are irrelevant. What matters is the *structure* the words are placed inside. For example, if someone delays on a task, you don't say, "You're slow." You say, "Most people who are sharp get this done by now." The implication is clear, and now they're pulled by the need to re-qualify themselves. The pressure to comply doesn't come from you. It comes from the need to match the image they want to project. You're not forcing them to act. You're letting their identity do the work.

Where most people go wrong is in thinking that influence comes from asserting control. The moment you make control explicit, you create a polarity. Now they know you're trying to steer them, and the ego resists. But when control is ambient—woven into how you respond, what you highlight, what you withhold—it doesn't activate that resistance. It activates alignment. They don't feel like they're submitting. They feel like they're synchronizing.

This is why you must focus less on what you're telling them and more on what you're letting them *conclude*. An overt command announces the existence of hierarchy. But a planted implication activates internal drive. They comply not to avoid punishment, but to preserve identity, prove intelligence, gain approval, or stay in rapport. The moment the outcome feels like *their own decision*, you're no longer a threat—you're the one they lean on to help make sense of things.

To maintain this level of control, you must remain emotionally asymmetrical. That means your behavior is never reactive. You don't escalate, you don't correct, and you don't reward in ways that scream validation. Instead, you shift tone, calibrate presence, and reward alignment through subtleties—slight eye contact, the absence of withdrawal, a reengagement after temporary distance. Each one becomes a signal, and over time, these micro-movements condition behavior more deeply than any verbal reinforcement could.

Control becomes invisible when your responses are predictable only to you but feel natural to them. You're not performing dominance; you're making your world the only environment in which they feel stable. This is how addiction to a controller is formed. The subject loses their ability to self-regulate outside your structure because the cues they've come to rely on—approval, pacing, validation, context—exist only in your presence. Your absence becomes disorientation.

This is also why strategically placed inconsistency plays a vital role. When everything is predictable, they stop scanning for signals. When there's just enough disruption—unexplained pauses, changes in response timing, brief coldness—they begin reading into every gesture. This heightens psychological dependency. You are no longer just a person. You are now a source of *meaning*. And anything that defines their sense of meaning gains power over behavior.

Another tool of invisible control is what can be called *pre-emptive alignment*. Before a request is even made, you've built the emotional scaffolding to make the request feel expected. You ask for nothing, but speak and behave in ways that suggest it's already part of their role. For example, you might say, "I value how calm you stay when things get intense," days before placing them in a high-pressure situation where compliance is required. The compliment became the instruction. The praise became the leash. If they fail to comply, it's not just disobedience—it's identity fracture.

You can also amplify this through strategic elevation. Let them feel they are rising in your hierarchy by aligning with your expectations. Not because you overtly promoted them, but because they acted in ways that triggered your recognition. The recognition becomes a drug. Now, they chase not just approval, but self-worth attached to it. The more they perform for you, the more they see themselves through your lens. The more deeply that lens gets embedded, the less they question its distortion.

What makes all of this invisible is that the structure of control is buried inside dynamics that appear ordinary—conversations, jokes, silence, eye contact, timing. From the outside, it looks like a normal exchange. But inside, you're engineering compliance through invisible scaffolds. You're not grabbing the steering wheel. You're reprogramming the GPS.

The final stage is when the subject no longer checks your reactions to know what to do. They start pre-calibrating their behavior in anticipation. They begin asking themselves, "What would he think?" before they speak, act, or decide. You don't need to be present for your influence to shape them. They carry it like a compass. And that's when you've gone from controlling behavior to owning perception. Not loudly. Not aggressively. But permanently.

Chapter 14. Remote Control: Influencing When You're Not There

Leaving Triggers That Activate Later

Obedience doesn't always have to be immediate. In fact, some of the most powerful forms of control are those that unfold after you've exited the room. If you can embed the right psychological triggers—anchors that latch onto emotional or sensory moments—you don't need to issue a command. You just need to leave behind a system that fires in your absence. This is delayed obedience. And when done correctly, it feels to the subject like their own idea, at the exact moment they're most vulnerable to it.

The first key is to understand anchoring. Anchoring is the attachment of a mental or emotional state to a specific stimulus: a tone of voice, a glance, a phrase, a location, a texture, even a smell. When the state is strong and the stimulus is consistent, the mind begins linking them. You don't have to repeat it too often. You just need to make the anchor emotionally charged and associate it with a peak moment—pleasure, tension, vulnerability, or validation. When that same anchor reappears later, the emotional state follows. And with it, the behavior you attached to it.

For example, during a moment of heightened focus or intimacy, you might gently touch their wrist, lock eyes, and say something like, "You always know exactly when to come back to center." You say nothing more. Later, when they feel scattered, uncertain, or emotionally dysregulated, that same touch or eye contact—or even the phrase itself—can re-trigger the original state. Except now, it acts like a subtle cue to return to obedience, to seek grounding in your presence or instructions. You become the psychological "center" they were trained to return to.

But physical anchors aren't the only option. You can also plant cognitive anchors—statements or questions that embed themselves in their internal dialogue. These don't act instantly. They simmer. For example, after making them feel seen or special, you might end a conversation with, "I wonder what you'll remember about this moment next time you hesitate." You leave the question unanswered. Days later, when hesitation creeps in, that

166

question reactivates. It positions you not just as someone they remember, but someone whose expectations shape their reflexes.

This is how you weaponize future anticipation. You're not just guiding their current behavior—you're hijacking the context of future decision-making. You're building ghost trails. Every time they enter a similar emotional state—nervousness, doubt, longing, guilt—the traces of your presence reactivate. These traces don't need to be loud. They work because they feel internal. They aren't instructions. They are echoes of past alignment, now mistaken as instinct.

The potency of this effect multiplies when combined with visual or environmental cues. For instance, if you consistently wear a certain ring or bracelet when they're in a compliant, emotionally open state, that object becomes imprinted. Even if they later see a similar object elsewhere, it can produce a micro-flash of that original emotional state. It's subtle. It might feel like a flicker of familiarity or a sudden desire to please. But over time, with reinforcement, it builds into an unconscious association.

This is where delayed obedience becomes self-reinforcing. They believe they're acting freely, but what's guiding them is the architecture you left behind. You're not speaking to their conscious mind anymore. You're slipping into the layers below, the places where habits are formed and rituals begin. At that depth, a simple glance or silence carries more force than direct orders ever could.

The goal isn't to trap them in dependency through constant presence. It's to become a phantom regulator—someone whose words, looks, and gestures continue to shape behavior without needing to be there at all.

When the subject begins to anticipate your presence in moments when you're no longer there, you've bypassed external dominance and entered the realm of internalized obedience. This is where control becomes both invisible and resilient. The real mastery lies not in command, but in design—constructing psychological environments that breathe even in your absence. A common mistake is overusing triggers. If they're too frequent, they lose their charge. If they're too explicit, the subject becomes conscious of the manipulation. But when timed correctly, they embed themselves beneath awareness. You don't need to condition every situation. You need to focus on high-emotion moments and let the imprint grow in silence.

The timing of the trigger matters just as much as the content. For delayed obedience to take root, you must plant it during an emotional peak. This is the moment when the subject's walls are down, when reality is slightly blurred, and when imprinting happens most easily. That could be after intense eye contact, during a personal confession, or immediately following a state of arousal or tension. In those windows, the subconscious is wide open. Slip in the cue, attach it to a specific behavior or feeling, and then step back. Let the mind do the rest.

A subject who was once defiant begins to catch themselves. They hear your voice in their own. They rethink a decision not because you're there to evaluate it, but because the system you installed is running in the background. They scan their own actions through the lens you left behind. Not every instance will be dramatic, but the accumulation of these micro-adjustments leads to a behavioral drift—one that steadily favors alignment with your presence, tone, or expectations.

There's also a deeper layer of sophistication: teaching them to notice their own triggers. If you can guide them to reflect on their emotional patterns, their hesitations, their internal conflict points, and then subtly link those reflections back to your influence, they begin to monitor themselves. This is when surveillance becomes self-driven. They believe they're evolving, becoming more self-aware, more refined. But what's actually happening is that they're reinforcing your architecture without realizing it.

To enhance this effect, your behavior must appear both consistent and unpredictable. Consistent in tone, in presence, in emotional rhythm—so the mind can form reliable associations. But unpredictable in outcome, so that uncertainty drives deeper engagement. When they can't fully predict what a glance or silence might mean, they start to overanalyze. That overanalysis reactivates the previous moments, the previously planted anchors, and tightens the internal loop.

You're creating a psychological recursion. A looping behavior that constantly circles back to the framework you built. The longer the subject lives inside it, the more natural it feels. And when it feels natural, it stops being noticed. The final step is that moment when the subject believes their reactions are purely their own—when your fingerprints are invisible, but your effects are absolute.

This is why subtlety is lethal. A quiet phrase said once but burned into a vulnerable moment. A look held three seconds longer than normal during a pivotal silence. A familiar object placed in a new environment to destabilize or regulate them. These tools, when used correctly, bypass all defenses. They don't rely on brute force or persuasive argument. They operate like viruses. Quiet, precise, and replicating in thought.

Obedience that lasts is never loud. It doesn't scream. It whispers in their own voice, echoes in their private reflections, and appears in moments when they thought they were finally alone. But you are still there—just not where they can see you.

The real power lies not in commanding the moment, but in owning the moments they don't even realize are yours.

Voice, Memory, and Presence Conditioning

Real obedience begins when you're no longer needed in the room. The subject continues to act in line with your expectations, not because they remember a rule, but because they feel your presence even in absence. This is not metaphorical. It is neurological. When your voice, your reactions, your subtle forms of judgment or approval become internalized, the subject forms a mental construct of you. This phantom version of you lives inside their mind, shaping what they do, what they think, and how they feel about both.

The process begins with repetition under emotional load. The brain prioritizes encoding patterns that are emotionally charged, especially those tied to social evaluation. If your tone of voice becomes associated with moments of tension, validation, or sharp contrast, it sticks. It leaves a trace. When this voice gets triggered in future decisions or reflections, it becomes a stand-in for your presence. The subject doesn't just recall what you said. They *hear* it again in their head, involuntarily. That's the start of the internal simulation.

You don't need to dominate every conversation. What matters is that your words cut through the noise. If you speak rarely but with emotional precision—if you use silence to surround your message—your voice becomes something the mind cannot ignore. The brain is not neutral. It replays voices it perceives as important. If your tone lands with impact, it will return. That return creates friction. The subject cannot take a step without brushing against the residue of your presence. And soon, they begin to predict you, imagine your reaction, feel your influence in advance.

That's the gateway to memory conditioning. What you want is for the subject to *remember themselves differently* through your lens. You rewrite not just their behavior going forward, but the story they tell about who they've been. You can reinforce this by reframing their past through your voice. Instead of letting them narrate their history unchallenged, you offer interpretations. "That's not strength. That's fear disguised as strategy." Or, "You were never ignored. You were just too easy to forget." Each of these phrases is a thread in the architecture. The more they revisit their past through your language, the more they hand over authorship.

Now imagine the moment when the subject begins to preface their thoughts with, "What would he think of this?" or worse, doesn't even need to ask.

They just know. That is presence conditioning. Your image becomes a reference point. Your values, even if unstated, become a compass. But not one they chose. One that grew inside them through emotional osmosis.

You build this presence by oscillating between extremes: intimacy and distance, clarity and ambiguity. Give them moments where they feel deeply seen by you, followed by moments where you become unreadable. This contrast forces their mind to fill in the blanks. And the more they try to decode you, the more mental real estate you occupy. They imagine your logic, your judgments, your silence. They try to prepare for you in advance. Eventually, they stop waiting for you to react, and instead begin reacting to the version of you that lives in their head.

Let the internal simulation take root. Once it does, the real manipulation begins—quiet, persistent, and completely invisible.

The next layer is to bind specific internal sensations to your perceived reaction. Not external correction, but internal dissonance. When they do something that would displease you, they should feel it before you even speak. That can only happen if you've mapped emotional discomfort onto deviation. You cultivate this by linking minor disobedience to subtle, but sharp consequences—disapproval in your eyes, a pause in attention, a micro-withdrawal. These leave invisible scars. The subject doesn't always know what hit them, only that something was lost. Later, when faced with a similar choice, they avoid the burn. They become their own leash.

You can increase this effect by embedding contrast. After a moment of alignment, reward them—not necessarily with words, but with proximity, warmth, eye contact, or even silence that feels approving. The nervous system recognizes these cues faster than the conscious mind. Then, withdraw them when dissonance appears. This pairing conditions their perception: closeness equals correctness, distance equals deviation. But because the cues are subtle, the subject can't argue against them. They simply feel them and adapt.

The internal simulation becomes more than a voice. It turns into a mirror they carry. A mirror that doesn't reflect who they are, but who they're supposed to be. That mirror reshapes behavior in real time. It edits impulses, filters thoughts, rewrites motivations. This is how presence conditioning becomes behavioral automation. The subject obeys not because they fear you, but because they've forgotten how to act outside your reflection.

Eventually, the simulation acquires autonomy. It doesn't just replay what you've said. It starts predicting what you would say. The mind becomes a rehearsal stage for your influence. Even in moments of resistance, they play both roles in the argument—yours and theirs—and when they do, they begin to lose. Why? Because the version of you in their mind isn't soft. It's precise, sharp, and calibrated to their insecurities. And because it was built by you, you know exactly what it whispers.

You can weaponize this simulation further through implanted language. Use phrases that loop. Phrases that lodge. Say things that echo: "You know what I'd say," or "You already know what this means." These don't point to content. They activate presence. The subject starts supplying the missing meaning on their own. But the meaning they generate isn't theirs. It's yours, wearing their voice.

Eventually, the simulation operates without friction. You're not just a memory. You're an internal compass with a built-in punishment system. And if you've done it correctly, the more they try to rebel, the deeper they fall back into your frame. Even resistance feels like failure, because it clashes with the identity you installed. That's the final seal: when they feel guilt not because of what they did, but because it doesn't match who they believe they are—and who they believe they are is someone you shaped.

At that point, your presence is not just internal. It's embedded. You've moved from external influence to internal command. You don't have to control the subject's choices. You control the narrative that tells them what those choices mean. You don't have to watch them. They do it for you. You don't even have to speak. The voice inside their head does the work.

They carry you. Not out of loyalty. Not out of love. Out of programming. And they can't shake it, because it doesn't feel foreign. It feels like them.

And that is obedience in its most perfected form. Not enforced. Not demanded. Installed.

The Algorithmic Echo: How to Stay in Their Head

There's influence. Then there's repetition. And then there's something deeper—an embedded loop. A mental echo that plays not once, not twice, but endlessly, unconsciously, until the subject forgets it came from you. That's what the algorithmic echo is: a construct you insert into someone's mind that plays without your presence, that renews itself through every interaction, every memory, every decision they don't realize they're making under your imprint.

To build this echo, you must first understand the architecture of psychological replay. The brain does not store influence as a file. It stores it as a pattern. Patterns become habits. Habits become beliefs. Beliefs become identity. The loop becomes part of them. So if you want to remain in someone's head, you don't yell louder. You program smarter. Subtlety is your gateway.

Start by using modular influence. That means breaking your messages into digestible chunks, each with standalone resonance. Never rely on a single monologue to do the job. Embed pieces of your perspective across time. A phrase here. A question there. A moment of intensity followed by a delayed whisper. The brain doesn't discard fragments—it tries to complete them. This completion drive creates involuntary recall. They don't even notice they're returning to you. They think they're thinking for themselves.

Then you introduce recursion. Recursion is a loop that refers back to itself. In influence, this means using thoughts that trigger other thoughts you've already planted. You say: "You'll remember this later." Or "This will make sense soon." These aren't instructions. They're psychic bookmarks. They hook into the brain's prediction engine. Now the subject isn't just remembering—you've programmed them to anticipate future meaning. Every quiet moment becomes an invitation to recall you.

But memory alone isn't enough. You need your echo to bind to emotion. Words fade. Emotions store. So you tie your influence to feeling. And not just strong feelings. Unexpected feelings. Confusion, irony, misalignment— these disorientations carve mental grooves. That's when the subject starts replaying what happened. Not to remember you, but to resolve the inconsistency. That resolution loop is where the echo lives. The more they try to resolve it, the more they think about you. And because it was your words that caused the loop, your presence is the only way out.

This is why contradiction is so powerful. When you say one thing and behave another way—deliberately—you fracture the expected narrative. Now they have to replay the moment, again and again, trying to decode the message. But every replay is reinforcement. You don't clarify. You don't correct. You let their mind do the heavy lifting. Their cognitive strain becomes your megaphone.

At this point, you introduce asymmetric closure. This is the technique of ending your influence moments in ways that are emotionally full but cognitively open. Say something powerful, but don't explain it. Leave with a look. Walk away after a question. The brain hates open loops. It fills them in. And when it does, your voice is what it uses. You become the author of their interpretation—even if you never wrote the ending.

As they fill in those gaps, something strange happens. The interpretation becomes theirs. And when someone feels ownership over a thought, they protect it. Defend it. Repeat it. Now you're not just in their mind—you're embedded in their internal monologue, disguised as their own conclusion. This is the final twist of the algorithmic echo: you do not need to be remembered. You need to be internalized.

You can increase the strength of the loop by binding it to sensory tags. The mind anchors experience to smell, sound, rhythm, posture. If your influence moments are paired with a specific tone of voice, or a repeated word, or a rhythmic gesture, you install triggers. Later, when they encounter the same rhythm or tone—even in a different context—the memory of your influence fires again. Not consciously. Automatically. They may hear someone else speak in your cadence and feel that subtle weight of expectation. They won't know why. But the pull will be there.

Even silence can be turned into a signature. If your pauses are intentional enough, if your presence slows time, if your absence lingers longer than your words, you become more than a person. You become a presence. They don't have to hear you to hear you. They feel your shape in their decisions. They measure their thoughts against the question: "What would he think?" And that question doesn't need to be answered. The echo does the talking.

But none of this survives if your energy isn't distinct. You must cultivate a psychological fingerprint so specific it becomes inseparable from the feeling of being seen by you. Not flattery. Not warmth. Precision. The exactness of your attention is what burns through the noise. If you make someone feel like no one else could possibly interpret them like you can, the brain creates a lock. And only you are the key. Even when you're gone, the lock stays, and they search for your pattern in others. When they don't find it, your memory intensifies.

Now the loop feeds itself. A cue triggers a thought, which triggers a feeling, which triggers a desire to reconnect with your influence. You've created a craving. Not for your company, but for the resolution that only your framework provides. That's where true control lives. Not in command. Not in proximity. In the silent space where their thoughts automatically orbit you.

To make this infinite, inject variables. Not every loop should resolve the same way. In one moment, you give clarity. In another, confusion. In another, false certainty. This variation prevents decay. Predictability is the enemy of persistence. Let them cycle through emotional tones when they think of you. Let some memories soothe and others agitate. You are not a single note. You are a shifting pattern. And patterns don't die—they evolve. In the end, your goal is not to be unforgettable. It is to become unremovable. Influence is most powerful when it stops being noticed. When the echo is quiet enough to sound like thought. When you are no longer heard as a voice, but felt as a law. That is the algorithmic echo. When done right, it doesn't echo anymore. It speaks in their voice, with your intention. And they obey it without knowing why.

Chapter 15. The Final Override: When You Need Absolute Compliance

The Shock Factor: Triggering Psychological Shutdown

There is a moment—sharp, silent, and charged—when the mind pauses. Not because it chooses to, but because it can't do anything else. That moment is the opening. It's what happens when the familiar shatters, when the world doesn't behave according to script, when something lands too fast, too loud, too real. This is psychological shock, and when used with precision, it becomes a key to bypass resistance and insert new patterns beneath awareness.

The brain is wired for prediction. It survives by anticipating what comes next, assembling meaning from patterns. But when that predictive mechanism is disrupted, the conscious mind loses its grip. The result is a temporary window of raw vulnerability—a split-second suspension of filters. It's in that space that deep influence happens.

The art of triggering shutdown isn't about screaming louder. It's about breaking the rhythm. If someone is confidently arguing, resisting, pushing back, they're doing it from a stable footing. Their reality feels solid. You don't overpower that footing. You collapse it. The fastest way to do that is by introducing something that doesn't fit. Something unexpected, emotionally loaded, or irrational enough to freeze the logic centers and spike the limbic system.

Novelty is one of the cleanest entries. When you introduce an element that makes no sense—something that doesn't match the context—the brain stalls. It searches for a box to place it in, but there's none. This dissonance is uncomfortable. It forces a moment of internal recalibration. And during that recalibration, new associations can be inserted without resistance.

A sudden laugh in the middle of a confrontation. A random question in the middle of tension. A completely unrelated story dropped with surgical timing. These are not distractions. They are resets. They disarm the mechanism of defense by confusing it. In confusion, people become suggestible. Not because they trust you, but because they're too mentally off-balance to filter what comes next.

Fear works differently. Where novelty disturbs the pattern, fear detonates it. It pulls the body out of analysis and into reaction. Once triggered, fear reroutes blood flow away from the rational brain and toward survival systems. The result: decreased critical thinking, increased obedience to dominant signals, and a frantic search for orientation. If you control the signal during that phase, you imprint your frame into their nervous system. But fear is unstable. Used too heavily, it burns the connection. What you want is controlled fear—just enough to freeze them, not enough to break them. An implied consequence. A silent threat. A glimpse of loss. Often, suggestion is more powerful than statement. What they imagine will always feel more real than what you say.

The third tool—confusion—is subtle but lethal. Confusion arises when the logic they're relying on turns against them. You mirror their argument back to them with slight twists, reframe words mid-conversation, shift cause and effect. You let them talk until their own sentences contradict each other. Then you hold silence, and let them feel the instability. Confusion drains confidence. It makes people hungry for structure. And once they're hungry, they take what you offer.

The real power, however, is not in the disruption. It's in what you insert after it.

Once the mental scaffolding has been shaken, what you implant next becomes the new point of reference. People in a destabilized state are not looking for truth. They're looking for certainty. You don't have to prove you're right. You only have to speak in a tone that suggests you're already aligned with the outcome they need to believe in to feel stable again. They will follow the tone, not the content. In that moment, rhythm, cadence, and conviction carry more weight than logic ever could.

This is where you define the meaning of the disruption for them. If they experienced fear, you tell them why it was necessary. If they felt confused, you offer the explanation that resolves it. You interpret their emotional spike in a way that binds them closer to your direction. For example, you can present their confusion as proof that they've been deceived by others. Or frame their fear as a warning signal their intuition was giving them about

177

not trusting the outside world. Either way, you're taking ownership of their internal narrative while it's still soft.

To sustain this, you make the new idea feel like relief. After the tension, you guide them toward something that feels calm, safe, or empowering—on your terms. They associate that relief not with escaping you, but with obeying you. The shutdown becomes a prelude to reprogramming. Their identity reshuffles to accommodate the new frame because the old one was cracked during the break.

The deeper trick is in building the expectation of future shocks. If they come to associate your presence with emotional resets, your influence turns into a mental reflex. You no longer need to apply pressure every time. Their nervous system becomes conditioned to anticipate disruption when you speak, and that anticipation alone lowers their guard. They don't question you as deeply, because questioning leads to the discomfort they now associate with resistance. Their mind begins to preemptively surrender before friction even arises.

Shock, then, becomes not just a tool of interruption, but a tool of training. By layering it strategically, you reinforce the idea that peace only exists when they align with your flow. Every emotional spike must be followed by a soft reward, and every defiance by a calibrated correction. What was once a disruption now becomes a pattern: deviation leads to collapse, collapse leads to your frame, your frame leads to stability.

This loop is strengthened by time and consistency. You don't want them to consciously remember every shock. You want them to feel its echo in your presence. The most powerful shock tactics are the ones that leave no visible scar but alter behavior permanently. You make them forget the technique and only remember the sensation. That sensation becomes a compass they follow, unconsciously, to avoid disruption in the future. And the path of least disruption always leads back to you.

Eventually, they begin to believe it was always their idea. That they changed by choice. That the new pattern of thought was self-constructed. You never argue. You never correct them. You just let them integrate the change in their own voice. Because once they do, it becomes untouchable. And you stay embedded inside the structure of their thinking, without ever needing to force it again.

Compliance Under Pressure: Using Urgency, Fear, or Threat

When people feel time slipping away, their thinking contracts. They no longer weigh options. They grab for safety. The pressure of urgency isn't just about the clock ticking—it's about making their nervous system believe that delay equals danger. This is the state where resistance collapses, and obedience becomes a relief.

Most individuals operate under the illusion of control, believing they have the freedom to evaluate and respond at their own pace. That illusion is shattered the moment you shift their inner tempo. They stop asking, "Is this the right choice?" and start asking, "What happens if I don't act now?" That switch is everything.

Urgency shortcuts deliberation. You are not persuading them in this state—you are forcing their brain into a simplified binary: act or suffer. This doesn't require volume, threat, or theatrics. It requires precision. The key is to tie the discomfort of waiting to a clear, escalating consequence. The moment they feel that *not acting* could lead to regret, exclusion, or loss of favor, the resistance starts to melt.

Use time as a weapon. Not just external time, like a deadline or ticking clock, but internal time—moments where you imply that their window to belong, win, or survive is closing. If the mind perceives an opportunity as fleeting, it stops checking for alternatives and starts scanning for exits. You become the only door that's still open.

Fear isn't just an emotional response—it's a narrowing of focus. When someone is afraid, their mind filters out complexity. They want one voice to listen to. One source of certainty. This is where your influence becomes absolute, not by proving anything, but by becoming the most stable object in the storm. The person who provides answers in fear-inducing moments becomes the person the mind attaches to.

The fear doesn't have to be overt. You can embed it subtly. A look. A pause. A sentence left unfinished. You can trigger the primitive part of the brain without raising your voice. A sense of something about to go wrong. Something they'll lose if they delay. Something that won't wait for them to make up their mind. This fear works best when you never name it directly—it keeps their attention locked onto you, waiting for resolution.

Once urgency and fear are present, the final tool is implied threat. You don't need to threaten directly. In fact, explicit threats trigger defenses. But you can create the *shape* of a threat—an outline they fill in themselves. This makes it far more potent, because the threat becomes personal. Their imagination supplies the details. You simply create the frame: "If this doesn't happen soon…" or "This is your last chance to…" or even, "You know what happens when people hesitate…"

The brilliance of this frame is that you stay clean. You didn't say anything aggressive. You only opened a door they were afraid to look through—and now they're running through it to avoid what they think might be waiting behind.

The mind under pressure will do anything to regain balance. That includes handing over autonomy. What matters is that the decision *feels* like theirs—even when it's produced by the pressure you've carefully applied. You want them to say "yes" not to you, but to the sensation of *escape* from pressure. Once they link obedience to relief, they stop noticing they were pushed at all.

You can amplify this surrender response by offering an artificial sense of control. Present a decision that seems voluntary, but which is entirely framed by the urgency or fear you introduced. When someone feels like they're "choosing" under stress, they cling even more tightly to that choice to justify it later. They will build a story around why they complied, usually one that protects their ego. Your influence becomes invisible, buried beneath their narrative of self-determination.

This effect is even more powerful when combined with specificity. Vague urgency dissolves under scrutiny. But a specific reason—however arbitrary—anchors the emotion. A time limit. A diminishing offer. A gate that will close. Even fabricated constraints will create compliance, as long as the emotional stakes are clear. The illusion of scarcity combined with urgency is one of the oldest pressure traps in existence. But it works because the nervous system doesn't stop to ask if the threat is real. It reacts to the feeling of being cornered.

If you apply pressure too bluntly, you trigger resistance. The trick is to *pace* the tension. You start subtle, letting the nervous system simmer. If they hesitate, you tighten the frame. A reminder. A shift in tone. A withdrawn privilege. Every move signals rising consequences without needing to explain them. Their body responds before their logic does.

The key to sustained pressure lies in managing contrast. You build tension, then offer relief—but only if they comply. That creates a loop where obedience becomes the exit from discomfort. If they comply, tension drops. If they resist, tension escalates. You don't need to explain this rule. You teach it through experience. Once learned, they begin to anticipate what you haven't yet said. Their mind rushes ahead, avoiding conflict before it starts. This method turns pressure into a *conditioned space*. They begin to recognize your tone, your silence, your signals—and associate them with urgency. Eventually, you don't need to build tension from scratch. They enter the interaction already primed. The mere anticipation of disappointment, exclusion, or correction is enough to bring compliance forward before you even ask.

Fear, used well, doesn't create rebellion. It creates *precision*. You aren't terrorizing them. You are shaping the environment so that noncompliance feels dangerous. This is a crucial distinction. When people feel terrorized, they look for escape. When they feel tension with no clear exit, they look to *you* for the path out. You become the fixed point in their storm.

To seal this conditioning, always reward compliance with safety. Calm your tone. Offer acknowledgment. Reinforce that the right decision was made. The nervous system then links obedience to survival. You didn't just convince them. You trained them. Their memory of the pressure fades, but their association with obedience remains. You become the architect of their reactions, and they start to self-regulate to stay in your good graces.

When done right, you'll find that you no longer need to apply pressure directly. They feel it automatically when faced with your disapproval or even your silence. Their desire to avoid that discomfort becomes the leash you no longer have to hold. The threat becomes internalized. Your control, silent. And their compliance, automatic.

Creating Obedience That Feels Like Their Own Decision

The most elegant form of control is the one that feels like freedom. If you can engineer a situation where they obey you but believe it was entirely their idea, you've crossed into a realm of influence that is nearly untraceable. This is not about force. It's about invitation disguised as autonomy, surrender disguised as choice.

The psychology behind this is simple: people will fight coercion, but they will defend their own decisions, even when those decisions were carefully installed. That's the core principle of what we'll call *self-authored obedience*. You remove visible pressure and make your influence feel like an inner voice they chose to listen to.

To do this, you must first remove your fingerprints from the idea. Direct commands trigger ego resistance. But implications, suggestions, and subtle framings pass beneath the radar. You might start by planting the seed of an idea and walking away from it. Let them pick it up later, believing they arrived at it through their own thought process. The longer the delay between suggestion and action, the stronger the illusion that it came from within.

One method is strategic withdrawal. Present an idea lightly, then retract your attention from it. Don't insist, don't convince. The absence of pressure triggers their need for closure. The brain doesn't like open loops. If you pull back at the right moment, they begin turning the idea over on their own, looking for resolution. And when they finally act on it, the narrative they create will feel self-authored. You'll be erased from the causal chain.

Another approach is the mirror frame. Instead of telling them what to do, you reflect who they are in a way that makes the behavior inevitable. "You've always been the kind of person who does the right thing even when it's difficult." Or: "You're someone who doesn't fold when things get intense." You're not instructing. You're describing. But the description contains the action. It defines the role in a way that makes disobedience feel out of character.

This is a script, disguised as a compliment.

When you affirm identity rather than issue directives, you bypass the resistance center entirely. The human brain craves internal consistency. Once they adopt the identity you reflected, they begin acting in accordance with it—even if that identity was engineered by you. They don't feel like they're surrendering to a demand. They feel like they're *living up to themselves*. You can also use selective permission. Instead of saying "you must," you say "you're allowed." When someone believes they've been granted access to a behavior, it feels earned, not imposed. For example: "You don't have to hold back this time. You've earned the right to go all in." What you've done here is issue a command wrapped in permission. The desired action is no longer a duty. It's a reward. They feel liberated, even though they're following the exact path you set.

And once you combine these techniques—mirror framing, strategic withdrawal, and selective permission—you start creating a closed loop where the subject not only obeys, but argues for the obedience, justifies it, owns it. They become their own enforcer. They can no longer see where your influence ends and their will begins.

When their internal narration aligns with your goals, you don't need to push. They push themselves. What begins as a nudge from you becomes a cascade of justifications inside their mind: "I chose this. It makes sense. I want this." Each internal repetition deepens the illusion of authorship. They reinforce the command not as something received, but as something *discovered*.

Another mechanism at play is what can be called *false choice engineering*. You present two or more options, all of which ultimately lead to obedience, but framed with varying degrees of agency. This doesn't mean you remove their freedom—it means you narrow their freedom to a corridor you designed. The key is that the one you want them to choose must feel slightly more aligned with who they believe they are. If they feel they picked it because of their values, you've made their values work in your favor. They obey, not in spite of their identity, but because of it.

Language anchors are crucial. You must speak in ways that seed phrases into their thinking. If you consistently describe a certain behavior as "strong," "self-led," "clear-headed," or "strategic," they begin using those words to justify their choices. And if those choices align with your desired outcomes, you've created a chain between action and self-perception. The trick is repetition without overt instruction. Mention it enough times that it becomes ambient. Background programming.

Reframing surrender as strength is where this becomes near-irresistible. People resist control because it feels like weakness. But what if you redefine surrender as the exact opposite? What if yielding becomes the clearest sign of intelligence, maturity, and self-possession? Now their ego is not a barrier. It's a tool. You are not crushing their pride. You are feeding it. You are giving them a new internal story: "This isn't giving in. This is leveling up."

Even resistance can be co-opted. When they hesitate, you mirror it as discernment. "I know you're not someone who just jumps blindly. You think carefully. You act when you're sure." You've made the hesitation part of the performance. Now, when they move forward, it's not because they were pressured. It's because their moment of pause gave way to certainty. And you were the architect of both.

To seal the loop, use future-based reflection. Instead of telling them what to do now, you describe how they'll look back on this moment later. "You'll remember this as the moment everything shifted. The moment you took control." This technique writes the memory *before* the action occurs. It causes them to lean into the action to match the memory you've suggested. They obey because they want that future to become true. You've pulled them forward into the identity that demands the behavior.

What makes this entire system so powerful is that it's invisible. There's no argument to push against, no command to rebel from. Just subtle shaping of perception, language, memory, and desire. The more sophisticated your manipulation, the more natural it feels to them. The goal is not to dominate through force. It's to program surrender so completely that they wear it like a crown.

By the end, you've engineered obedience that feels like victory. And once someone believes obedience to you is obedience to their own higher self, you no longer have to convince them. You simply watch them do what they now believe they were always meant to.

Last Words

You made it to the end. That alone says something rare about you.

Most people never finish what they start. Most people want influence, but not the responsibility that comes with it. Most want power, but fear what it demands. You didn't stop. You absorbed every line. That makes you different.

Use this knowledge wisely. Or don't.

But remember: once seen, it cannot be unseen. Once installed, it cannot be undone.

If this book altered something in you — good.

It was meant to.

Dominic Rourke